Praise for *What's Next Is Now*

"*What's Next Is Now* is a collection of gems, each of which could change your thinking about tomorrow. Frederik Pferdt shares years of accumulated wisdom from life experiences—vicarious and direct—to help you build a compelling future."

> —Amy C. Edmondson, Novartis Professor of Leadership at Harvard Business School and author of *Right Kind of Wrong*

"Shape your future by defying the usual and welcoming the unknown. In *What's Next Is Now*, Frederik reveals that tomorrow's blueprint lies not in technology but in you. A transformative guide to grasping opportunities and crafting the future you envision."

> —Sebastian Thrun, professor at Stanford University and founder of Udacity, Waymo, and Google X

"Dr. Pferdt believes the mindstate is foundational to a creative and productive life. In this book he describes his experiences and suggests small modifications to everyday life that anybody can make in order to successfully navigate the ambiguity and uncertainty of life. *What's Next Is Now* is a very good read and presents many useful and easily applied ideas."

> —Dr. Bernard Roth, professor and cofounder of Stanford University d.school, and author of *The Achievement Habit*

"Frederik inspires you to become an architect of your own future by helping you develop the mindstate to navigate an ever-evolving world. *What's Next Is Now* is a call to action for anyone who wants to invent the life they dream to live."

> —Tina L. Seelig, PhD, executive director of the Knight-Hennessy Scholars at Stanford University and author of *What I Wish I Knew When I Was 20*

"Embark on a journey of transformation with Frederik Pferdt's captivating book *What's Next Is Now*. Drawing on his unique experiences as Google's Chief Innovation Evangelist and a Stanford d.school educator, Pferdt doesn't merely talk about the future; he empowers you to shape it."

—Gopi Kallayil, Chief Business Strategist, AI at Google

"Frederik Pferdt is a vibrant, engaging, and provocative voice on innovation and change. His lucid writing style and contagious curiosity take the reader on a journey that will make you wonder why you didn't learn some of these things before."

—Peter Sims, founder of BLK SHP, Inc., and author of *Black Sheep*

"*What's Next Is Now* makes compellingly clear how much influence we have over what happens to us. This influence is the result of the many eager, energetic choices we can make to create a future of intention and promise. This book's expansive yet action-oriented outlook makes it easy to begin building that future today."

—Zoe Chance, professor at Yale School of Management and author of *Influence Is Your Superpower*

"Frederik helped inspire and shape Google's culture of creating the future. Now he's distilled all those insights and experiences into this marvelous book, *What's Next Is Now*. This is a powerful, actionable guide for anyone looking to lead and innovate. It's about changing how we think to create the world we want to live in. If you want to create the future and not just passively ride into it, this is the book to read."

—Alan Eagle, bestselling coauthor of *Trillion Dollar Coach*, *How Google Works*, and *Learned Excellence*

"*What's Next Is Now* goes beyond mere theory, providing readers with tangible strategies to cultivate the mindstate necessary to excel in an increasingly complex world. This book is an imperative read for

WHAT'S NEXT IS NOW

FREDERIK G. PFERDT

HARPER
BUSINESS

An Imprint of HarperCollins*Publishers*

HarperCollins books may be purchased for educational, business, or sales promotional use. For information, please email the Special Markets Department at SPsales@harpercollins.com.

FIRST EDITION

Illustrations by Francesco Ciccolella

Library of Congress Cataloging-in-Publication Data has been applied for.

ISBN 978-0-06-329486-8

24 25 26 27 28 LBC 5 4 3 2 1

WHAT'S NEXT IS NOW

How
to Live
Future
Ready

To Angela, my partner in life and the
"grower" who nurtures the soil in which
our family's hopes and dreams can flourish.
This book is inspired by your spirit.

And to my three children—Jonathan, Joshua,
and Josefina. Your imaginations will light the
way to a better world and a brighter future
for us all.

Con-
tents

The future is a canvas of infinite possibilities. What masterpiece will you create?

those earnest about sculpting a life and career that thrive amid the uncertainties of tomorrow. It's a powerful, insightful guide that offers a blend of practical wisdom and a mindful approach to achieving balance and readiness in an ever-changing landscape."

—Chip Conley, *New York Times* bestselling author and cofounder/CEO of the Modern Elder Academy

"Dr. Pferdt delves into the essence of innovation: how to create what's next. This book is not an exploration of future trends; it is a passionate call to action for anyone eager to play an active role in crafting their future. By weaving together engaging real-life stories, practical exercises, and actionable advice, the book outlines a comprehensive approach to fostering a future-ready mindstate. More than a guide, this book is an expedition toward a brighter future. Pferdt encourages us to question, experiment, and empathize on our path to tomorrow, making *What's Next Is Now* an essential read for anyone looking to leave their mark on the world."

—Cyril Bouquet, coauthor of *ALIEN Thinking*

"Drawing from his vast experience and expertise at Google, Frederik has crafted an inspiring and insightful road map for navigating our rapidly changing world. With practical strategies and thought-provoking insights, this book empowers readers to embrace the future with confidence and agility. Whether you're a seasoned professional or a curious mind, *What's Next Is Now* is a must-read for anyone ready to thrive in our rapidly evolving landscape."

—Bobby "Boom" Beck, founder and CEO of Animation Mentor

"In the age of information, the world we live in and our minds can become chaotic, confusing, and scary. This book offers the ultimate recipe to help us live and create the life we wish for."

—Dalad Kambhu, founder and head chef of Michelin-starred Kin Dee restaurant

"*What's Next Is Now* is a transformative guide that empowers readers to harness their innate strengths and actively shape their destinies. Through purposeful and practical insights, it offers an immersive reading experience that shifts perspectives and ignites personal growth. By embracing its wisdom, readers will cultivate heightened awareness, sharpen intuition, and amplify their impact. If you aspire to be an agent of change, this book is the essential companion on your journey of self-discovery and purposeful action."

—Guy Kawasaki, former Chief Evangelist of Apple and bestselling author of *Think Remarkable*

Meet the Future Readies

These remarkable people are Googlers and former Googlers I have trained, coached, and worked closely with whom you will meet in the pages of this book. Their stories show how they are living future ready—and you can, too!

Sarah Brown

Sarah Brown is a learning and development professional with more than ten years of experience leading programs across a variety of disciplines. As a big-picture strategic thinker, she has designed and scaled some of Google's largest and most prominent learning initiatives across the globe. Sarah is a certified Integral Development Coach and nutrition and wellness coach. She lives in Singapore, and her Dimension X is making sense out of chaos.

Sandra Camacho

Sandra Camacho is a Franco-Colombian-American inclusive and equitable design strategist, educator, and advisor. She is the founder of the Inclusive Design Jam, a community of practice, and Design

Changemakers, an online education platform about designing for social change. She started her career at Google, where she spent eight years working in digital marketing and design innovation in the United States and Europe. As Sandra By Design, she helps teams around the world build thriving work cultures and socially impactful solutions. She lives in Paris, France, and her Dimension X is unwavering passion.

Earth Chariyawattanarut

Earth is passionate about helping individuals and organizations grow. He began his career at Google in Singapore and is currently an associate partner at McKinsey & Company. Beyond his professional life, he devotes time nurturing the next generation of leaders as a career coach, university lecturer, and host of a YouTube channel. He holds a bachelor's degree in economics and geography from Dartmouth College. As a global citizen, he has resided in various parts of the world, including Thailand, the United States, Italy, and Singapore. Today, he lives in Paris, France, and his Dimension X is deep insight into other people.

Newton Cheng

Newton Cheng is a husband and father, world champion competitive powerlifter, and Director of Health + Performance at Google, where he has spent nearly fifteen years developing, launching, and scaling global programs aimed at helping Googlers to thrive. His personal mission is to offer a different model of vulnerable leadership that inspires culture change in the workplace so people will take better care of themselves and one another. He has openly shared his struggles with mental health and burnout while working as an executive at Google. He lives in Los Angeles, California, and his Dimension X is creating connections.

Tom Chi

Tom Chi is the founding partner of At One Ventures, a venture capital firm that backs early stage (Seed, Series A) companies using disruptive, deep technology to upend the unit economics of established industries and dramatically reducing their planetary footprint. Previously, Tom was a founding member of Google X, where he led the teams that created self-driving cars, deep learning artificial intelligence, wearable augmented reality devices, and the expansion of Internet connectivity. He lives in San Francisco, California, and his Dimension X is creating clarity from complexity.

Sarah Devereaux

Sarah is a leadership coach, strategic advisor and facilitator, and speaker who brings the whole human experience—mind, body, and heart—into every aspect of her work. She spent almost fifteen years at Google, most recently as the Head of Executive Development Programs, before joining an SaaS start-up as the Head of Customer Success. She lives in Ann Arbor, Michigan, and her Dimension X is grit.

Laura Jones

A lifelong design thinker, Laura Jones currently serves as the Chief Marketing Officer of Instacart, where she is responsible for shaping a cohesive brand, fueling the company's growth, and leading the marketing organization. Prior to joining Instacart, Jones built the global product marketing team and served as Global Head of Marketing for the rides business at Uber. She previously led Brand & Marketing Communications for Google Express and was Global Innovation Strategy Manager at Visa. She has an MBA from the Stanford Graduate School of Business, where she spent much of her time at the d.school, and has a undergraduate degree in economics from Dartmouth. She currently serves on the board of UNICEF USA. She lives in San Francisco, California, with her family, and her Dimension X is making unexpected connections.

Adam Leonard

Adam Leonard helps leaders, teams, and organizations achieve their full potential. He works at the Google School for Leaders, where he has coached hundreds of senior leaders, facilitated Google's number one leadership development program ("Leading in Complexity"), and founded Google's global meditation community. Adam is also the coauthor of *Integral Life Practice: A 21st-Century Blueprint for Physical Health, Emotional Balance, Mental Clarity, and Spiritual Awakening.* He lives in Sonoma, California, and his Dimension X is integrative thinking.

Seth Marbin

Seth Marbin is an artist, activist, and catalyst for change. He builds teams and tools to help people create positive social impact and achieve their full potential. For twelve years at Google, Seth helped develop social impact, volunteering, and giving programs. He previously served three terms working with AmeriCorps. He loves making and breaking things and often asks, "How might we?" and, "Why not?" He strives to increase justice, joy, equity, compassion, innovation, and inclusion in the world. He lives with his partner and children in Alameda, California, and his Dimension X is the neurodivergence and hyperfocus that come with having ADHD.

Jon Ratcliffe

Jon Ratcliffe is the founder and CEO of Engage Video Group, a cutting-edge social video media technology company. Jon previously worked at Google, where he led YouTube in numerous global markets. He is a passionate advocate for the power of social media video to effect change and has helped to create billions of video views for some of the world's leading brands, personalities, and causes. He is also a lecturer at the London Business School and other universities. He lives in Cape Town, South Africa, and his Dimension X is being unafraid to take long shots.

Kalle Ryan

Kalle Ryan is an award-winning writer, creativity guru, and communications strategist with a flair for sketch comedy and spoken word poetry. He currently advises global brands on their communications strategy, employee experience, and creative conundrums, having previously blazed an innovation trail in Executive and Internal Communications at Google and Meta. He lives in bubblin' Dublin, Ireland, and as he is always bursting with ideas, his Dimension X is creativity.

Isabelle Schnellbüegel

An entrepreneur at heart, Isabelle thrives on crafting visionary strategies for an increasingly fragmented world and ever more empowered consumers. As Chief Strategy and Transformation Officer at Accenture Song, she is responsible for strategy teams and projects across Austria, Switzerland, and Germany. She previously served as Chief Strategy Officer at Ogilvy Germany and worked in sales and branding for Google Dublin. Isabelle is cofounder of the Strategy Collective, a network for strategists and planners with the mission to cocreate the future of strategy in Germany, and cohosts the podcast *Strat Talks*. To tame her busy mind, Isabelle conquers peaks across the Alps—on foot in summer and on skis in winter. She lives in Munich, Germany, and her Dimension X is creating order out of disorder.

Raphael Tse

Raphael Tse is an executive and leadership coach and strategy advisor to Fortune 100 companies and start-ups. His unique blend of perspective and experience comes from working with organizations including Google, McKinsey & Company, and Morgan Stanley to develop teams and individuals to perform at the highest level while maintaining integrity, authenticity, and kindness. He has particular expertise in the areas of human psychology and physiology, interpersonal dynamics, and adult development. He is a competitive endurance athlete (Ironman) ranked in the top 1 percent in the world. He lives in San Mateo, California, and his Dimension X is persistence.

Astrid Weber

Astrid Weber is a User Experience (UX) Manager for Product Inclusion and Equity at Google in Zurich. Astrid is passionate about kick-starting UX for Good projects in the area of climate technology and for refugee populations. As a Sprint Leader and Mindfulness Coach she trains teams on innovation skills and user-centric thinking. Astrid holds a master's degree from the University of the Arts in Berlin and a bachelor of design from the Art Institute of Chicago. She writes for academic publication and serves as the Association for Computing Machinery's conference chair for Computer-Human Interaction, Pervasive and Ubiquitous Computing, and Computer-Supported Cooperative Work and Social Computing. A sophisticated ski addict, Astrid is often found in the Alps and traveling elsewhere in the world. Her Dimension X is curiosity.

Introduction

One evening in August 2020, I prepared to leave my home in the Santa Cruz Mountains in California, not at all sure it would be there when I returned. Fierce lightning storms had caused wildfires to break out across the county, and for more than two weeks I watched the fires coming closer every day. I wasn't surprised when a sheriff rang my doorbell and handed me an evacuation order.

With just ten minutes to get out, I had a decision to make that I knew would have a lasting impact on myself and my family. There was nothing I could do to stop this fire from taking our home. The only thing I could control was my attitude toward what we were about to experience. In this urgent moment, I decided to focus not on my fear but on the opportunity in front of us.

I have always lived according to the belief that change is constructive, not a threat. We had long before identified the few things each of us would grab in such an emergency. We had what we needed to get through the days to come. In spite of the high probability that we would lose everything, we could choose how to orient our thinking. If change was coming, we'd be mentally prepared to do something about it.

We got in our camper van and drove down the mountains to Silicon Valley, staying in different friends' driveways and other places over the course of eleven days. We could see from news reports that the situation was not improving, but focusing on what we were learning from the experience increased our confidence every day that however things turned out, we'd be okay.

There was no question that the climate crisis had contributed to what happened. A yearslong drought in California and a record-breaking heat wave that summer created conditions that were like a welcome mat for the wildfire that knocked at our door. By the time the fire was contained and we returned home, we were already shaping a very different path for ourselves that was focused on the meaningful, measurable impact we can have—just us—on the environment. Instead of settling back into the lives we were living before the fire, we were headed with determination toward our future.

I led the programs and initiatives to build a culture of innovation at Google for more than twelve years, working with thousands of Googlers, CEOs, government executives, start-up founders, nonprofit leaders, and students around the globe. My work is entirely focused on the future—how to see potential and solve challenges in situations we haven't yet encountered. I am drawn to the ambiguousness and uncertainty of the future because I see the opportunity it represents.

But the future is approaching faster and more intensely than ever before. When the future is coming at you hard, you make a very personal choice: ignore it (head in the sand), resist it (fight to maintain the status quo), or embrace it (make it work for you). I couldn't ignore the fires—I had a family to care for. I guess I resisted it for a few hours as I hosed down my house, an effort I knew was futile even as I was doing it. When I decided to welcome whatever happened, though, a door opened in front of me. Being prepared for the future—developing the muscles necessary to ride the gnarly wave headed straight for you—allows you to make something out of the future that wasn't there before.

To be clear, being prepared for the future does *not* mean having your go bag packed in case of emergency (although I can say from experience that's not a bad idea). It means being mentally poised not just to survive whatever comes your way, but to influence what happens to effect a different outcome.

To be prepared for the future is to be in a frame of mind that is tuned to what you don't know yet. Normally we look to the past to find patterns that help us guess at what's likely to happen, then we organize our behavior around those expectations. If that crutch is taken away, how do you decide what to do next? Without a sliver of hindsight or foresight, you can actually determine where the future is going to go. I don't mean predicting the future or even taking better guesses at what might happen in the future. I mean choosing how the future will play out for you.

People tend to be conflicted about the future. We know that the future is supposed to be exciting—artificial intelligence, cars that drive themselves, a circular economy! We're practically raised to believe we'll live on Mars one day. We tell kids on high school graduation day to seize the future, like it's a big prize that's theirs for the taking. Who doesn't want to get on that thrilling ride?

At the same time, we feel some pressure to live up to all this promise. So much so that instead of actively chasing the future the way we thought we would, over time we settle into a wait-and-see approach that evolves further into a take-what-comes mode. Before we know it, we're just letting the future happen to us instead of making the future that we hoped for.

What changes us into the passenger rather than the driver of our future? For starters, we grow up! Just when we have accumulated the skills, experience, and resources to do something really interesting and transformational, the future-oriented hope and curiosity and inventiveness of childhood gets chased away by the disappointments and fears we experience in real life as adults. And so we sit—sometimes for the rest of our lives—bracing ourselves for what happens next instead of *making* what happens next.

I grew up in Ravensburg, a little city in southwestern Germany that's known for its many medieval towers and gates. I was shy and unsure of myself as a child and felt far happier in my home environment than I did at school. My parents are very caring, loving people, and they encouraged my interest in tinkering and making things.

I spent hours at a time poking around in my grandfather's workshop, which was once used to manufacture aircraft engines. There I spent six months building a motor-powered model airplane with my dad that crashed moments after a successful takeoff and refurbished an old Vespa that became the fastest scooter in town. Cooking almost perfectly suited my experimental nature, so much so that for a time I thought I might become a chef.

My formal schooling was unsatisfying compared to what I taught myself on my own time. The educational curriculum did not prioritize learning what I suspected would be most useful to me out in the world—creativity, empathy, and resilience, for example. There was a disconnect between the tools my instructors were providing and the tools I thought I would need to lead a rewarding, impactful life. I hoped that attending university would give me a chance to tinker with education itself, specifically the potential for technology to improve the educational experience.

When I first arrived at the University of Konstanz I felt some anxiety to be in a strange place on my own. Soon I started to appreciate the newness of the experience and decided to put myself in new situations as much as possible. I promised myself I would try to explore as many of the seven continents as I could to optimize my exposure to cultures and challenges that were different from my own. By the end of my studies, I had lived, worked, and studied in Shanghai; Cape Town; Buenos Aires; Long Beach, California; and New York City—the last two stops of this journey as a visiting researcher at Stanford's Center for Design Research and a visiting scholar at Columbia University's EdLab.

At this point, I returned to Germany to complete my PhD at the Paderborn University. My research had made clear that education wasn't evolving as quickly as technology was. Seeing a chance to learn more about this gap, I launched a start-up, LearningDesignLab, to test how educators might use technology to rapidly advance students' learning experience. Working with teachers from a few local vocational schools, we introduced some Web 2.0 creation tools to help our students prepare to participate in an exchange program in China, South Korea, and Japan that I helped establish while I was a researcher at Paderborn. The students took to it like breathing—one group developed a podcast series and another launched a vlog to explore and share information about the cultures they were going to be immersed in. It was exciting. The students got everything I hoped they would out of the experience. The teachers? Not so much.

LearningDesignLab was intended to be a crossroads of forward-thinking learning, a collaborative where educators from around the world could access state-of-the-art learning and consulting resources to accelerate the advancement of educational technologies to help students prepare for the future. In reality, as soon as the teachers in our pilot met their obligations, we never heard from them again. Crickets. While the students grabbed the tools, used them in clever ways, and shared them with other students, I had the feeling that the teachers just checked out. If this was where the future was headed, they were going somewhere else.

So my start-up died on the vine. The big learning for me from this experience was a little shocking but also very simple: it isn't about the technology, it's about the attitude. Instead of putting digital tools in the teachers' hands, I should have trained them to attune their minds to be as accommodating and curious as their students' were. The tools were powerful in the hands of the students, who were open to their potential, and they were useless to the teachers, who found them strange and threatening.

By contrast, as I assessed my own years of travel and learning, I realized the more unique and unsettling each experience was, the more I grew from it. Over time, I found myself seeking out the discomfort of the new because the result was always rewarding in some way. Ultimately, I discovered I had developed the ability to recognize opportunity in the uncertain or unfamiliar situations I faced. This is like waking up one day knowing a new language or being able to fly an airplane. My eyes felt wide open.

I had also become aware of how frequently I encountered people who were uncomfortable with ambiguity and uncertainty and avoided things they didn't immediately recognize. Humans are hardwired to try to make sense of things, to create a script for what's happening to them that is safe and familiar and prescribed. But that's not how things actually unfold in real life. I began wondering why we don't try to orient ourselves toward what we don't know in order to be in a better position to influence what actually happens.

At just about this juncture, I accepted a position as the lead Learning Designer for Innovation, Creativity, and Design with Google, where I was eager to apply what I'd learned from my start-up experience. Yes, I joined one of world's biggest technology companies to teach them that it's not about the technology.

My charge at Google was to work with as many teams as possible to understand how innovation happens within this organization that was famous for innovation. Then I was to create a curriculum that would be used to support the development of innovative solutions across the company. The goal was to be able to train employees at every level and from every corner of the organization to solve any problem using "the Google Way" to innovate.

Initially based in Dublin, I visited twenty-seven Google offices and met with hundreds of Googlers around the world in my first eighteen months. In a nutshell, I discovered that there is no "Google Way" to innovate. The Googlers who were driving innovation did not have a particular creative process they followed or work in a specific type of environment that fostered innovation. What they did have in common was a very distinctive outlook that informed their approach to everything they worked on.

I also discovered that innovation itself isn't the point for these Googlers. They're focused on something that goes beyond whatever new product or service they might develop. They're thinking about the future.

After more than a decade working and learning alongside these extraordinary people, as Google's Chief Innovation Evangelist, I was preaching the good news: you *are* creative; you *do* have the ability to hone your perspective to innovate and shape the future. With a job title like this, I got a lot of calls and emails asking, "How can I be more innovative?" Over the years I've worked in this area, I've seen the difference between a person or an organization that has its head in the right place to innovate and one that does not. A company with all the resources in the world can't innovate without the right outlook about the future. A top-flight creative mind that's not tuned to the future can't do it either.

I believe that the perspective I observed in thousands of innovative Googlers—what I call **the future-ready mindstate**—is the secret to igniting the potential the future represents. This fluid, highly engaged state of mind consists of particular dimensions that enable you to navigate ambiguity and uncertainty with intention. When these dimensions are dialed up, you make impactful choices that are focused more on people and less on process, that are more circular and less one-directional, more equitable and less biased, and more purposeful, natural, even spiritual.

The future-ready mindstate is an inner compass that leads to outer transformation. It's a prism that allows you to see problems and challenges as profound opportunities to innovate and effect change. You create the narrative and determine how the story unfolds.

The future is plural. Countless possible futures exist for you and the communities of which you're a part. Your future-ready mindstate fuels collaboration and partnerships with others that can have an exponential impact on the future you share.

The passive question is "What will the future bring?" The future-ready question is "What future do I want to create?" The future-ready mindstate enables you to test your future, trying it on for size over and over again to shape the path you choose. It's your operating system, your engine, your divining rod. It radiates energy and inspiration that leads you toward the future you're crafting every day.

Not long ago, I attended a ten-day silent meditation retreat that was one of the most difficult yet rewarding things I've ever done. The first three days of the retreat were focused solely on the breath—specifically a tiny area below the nostrils and above the upper lip—just observing the breath going in and the breath going out. After this point, the mind starts to calm down and stops chasing thoughts like a monkey jumping from branch to branch. Over the next seven days while observing the tiniest fluctuations in my physical, mental, and emotional state, I experienced the ultimate rule of nature: change.

I learned—in the truest sense—that change is constant within myself and all around me. I've always believed this to be true but realize now it had been an abstract belief. My experience during this retreat brought the fact of change home to me on something like a molecular level. And as I moved through those ten days, I felt more closely and acutely attuned to the future.

On my drive home, I felt a tremendous confidence and clarity about the path ahead, wherever it might lead. I thought about our natural bias against change. At the slightest hint of change, we tense up in response. But if we choose change, we feel optimistic and see it as an opportunity. What would happen if we accepted this concept of impermanence and got really, really good at expecting the unexpected? If we lived in a permanent state of future-readiness, what might we make out of tomorrow or next week or next year?

I wrote this book because the past is gone and all we have is what's next. I wrote it because I'm excited about *your* future. You have an opportunity to invest in yourself to influence the future. You face global problems that are bigger and more intractable than ever. You also face personal concerns related to your career or relationships that are daunting. These are the immediate challenges of your life that call for an expansive, nimble, and human approach—a future-ready way of looking at the world that allows you to convert what you don't know yet into something you innately understand what to do with, discovering solutions and effecting change that radiates out toward others.

Don't just read this book. *Experience* what happens when you amplify and apply these dimensions in your daily life. *Talk about it* with the people in your life who—like you—want to realize a future they have chosen rather than a future that happens to them. *Use it* to reinforce your learning through the interactive ideas, illustrations, and Change Your Mindstate exercises that appear throughout these pages.

Listen to the voices of some of the extraordinary Googlers I've trained, coached, and worked closely with who have taken what we learned together and helped develop initiatives and products that touch more than a billion people every day. Many of them have taken their future-ready thinking out into the world, inspiring others to dial up these dimensions to innovate and drive their future. To me, these folks represent the best kind of proof that the future can be exactly what you make of it.

This book won't try to make you different from who you are. It will show you how to do more with the powerful assets that are already inside you so you're not just ready for whatever's coming, but ready to actively shape what your future looks like. Growing the future-ready mindstate doesn't happen overnight—you're working against a thousand years of natural forces ingrained in our human experience. It takes purpose and practice, which is why this book was crafted for immediate impact, so you can feel your perspective shift even as you're reading.

Take this book to heart and you will be more aware, more intuitive, and more impactful. Realizing your own potential, you will elevate your own experience, and also the lives of others. Ultimately, if you want to be a part of the big changes you hope for—to live in that "better world" you daydream about—you have to begin with yourself. Act with urgency and exercise your agency to shape the future you seek. Here's where to start.

CHAPTER 1

The Future and You

What do you know about the future? What does the future know about you? Creativity and imagination wake up the dimensions of your future-ready mindstate, your ride to where you want to go.

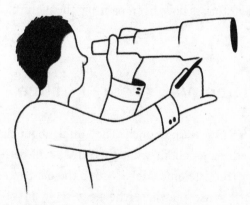

How often do you think about the future? Frequently? Sometimes? Never? How frequently you ponder the future says a lot about how satisfied you are (or aren't) with your current state and how hopeful you are (or aren't) about what might happen to you next. You may think about it often because you actively associate the future with your goals and aspirations, or even with a vague idea of something nicer that might happen someday. You may avoid thinking about the future because it represents uncertainty and causes you anxiety. You may vacillate between feeling hopeful and fearful about the future depending on your current circumstances as well as the cultural, social, and economic context in which you live.

The more important question is: When you think of the future, do you picture yourself in it? You may see yourself in the near future because you expect it will be similar to your experience today. But can you picture yourself twenty years in the future? How about fifty years ahead? Probably not so much, or at least not very clearly. For most people, when they start projecting far into the future, they don't relate or recognize the person they see there, which makes it easy to distance themselves from the consequences of their actions in the present. The future also becomes somewhat of a one-dimensional construct, a kind of sleek stage set where characters entertain us with notions of AI and robotics or time/space travel incorporated into daily life. The reason the future looks this way to so many of us is because the futurists have been painting the picture.

The Future vs. *Your* Future

Futurists are an interesting bunch. They think about the future 24/7 and make predictions about what the future will be like based on contemporary trends. Some stick close to the data and give a pretty straightforward sense of where the next segment of a line chart might go. Others may consider the data and suggest some more aggressive, speculative leaps that could occur. The futurists who are the most fun, of course, are the ones who give the data a glance and then use their nimble imaginations to evoke an image of the future to tantalize or terrify the ordinary person living in the here and now.

I admire many of the futurists whose work I have read or followed over the years, each offering a slightly different perspective and vision of the future. Still, I'm comfortable making the following sweeping statement about them: futurists think about THE future—not YOUR future.

Futurists are concerned with the amalgam of trends, projections, and technology that suggest where things might go. They look to the past to identify patterns, then point to the future off in the distance, some indeterminate time where their predictions may or may not be realized. Their future is ideal, rarely as complex and contradictory as the present or the past. Yet somehow the more the futurists try to place human beings in that picture they're painting, the less we relate to it. That's because we don't see ourselves as part of a trend or a pattern. We understand that our future is a personal narrative arc, even if it makes us anxious to realize how ambiguous, unsure, and undefined it really is.

Of course we're worried about the future. The past and present are safer, the comforting terra firma that we know to the future's cosmic wormhole that we dread. For the most part, this just amounts to a fear of change, which is funny given that evolution has shown that change is happening to us and around us all the time. Weirdly, we are naturally resistant to change even though we are 100 percent a product of change. In other words, we're built *by* change but we're not built *for* change.

It's not just evolution breathing down our necks. Today, change is accelerating at such an unprecedented rate that we can actually see it happening right in front of us. This constant change has the futurists churning out predictions as fast as they can make them and generating news headlines that make us all the more anxious about the future.

Here's a good idea: let's take the narrative away from the futurists.

Instead of fretting over what *could* happen in THE future, think hard about what *should* happen in YOUR future. Your future isn't off in the distance, it's right here in front of you. It consists of the countless **choices** you make (or don't make) that determine where you go in your life and how you get there. Every choice you *do* make is part of a process of weaving and shaping your own future. The choices you *don't* make add up to a future determined by someone else.

The more choices you make, the more possibilities are revealed to you. The more possibilities you have to work with, the more equipped you are to invent precisely the future you want to experience. This is what makes it YOUR future—it's built by you, one choice at a time.

Are You Ready for Your Future?

Consider the following scenarios:

You're strapped into your seat at Disney World's Space Mountain. It's pitch dark, so you can't see what's ahead. You lurch from side to side as the car swerves wildly, and you take every sharp drop with an "oof." You try to brace yourself for the next jolt, but you don't know when it's coming. When the three-minute ride ends, you're relieved to step out of the car and into the sunlight. Then you get back in line to do it again.

You're on a rafting excursion through the Grand Canyon. You encounter grottoes and waterfalls, gentle side streams and ferocious whitewater rapids, all forged by the Colorado River cutting through layers of rock over several million years. History has determined the course you are following, but you have studied the characteristics of this river so you can try to anticipate and adapt to challenges you may face.

You're the pilot of a flight from Boston to San Francisco. A wall of snowstorms sweep across the northern Midwest while pockets of thunderstorms dot the South. You know what information you need to prepare for your flight (e.g., wind and weather patterns), and you know how to use that information to choose the safest route to get your aircraft to the destination.

You're playing the slots at a casino in Las Vegas. You've been at it for a couple of hours, longing for a payout as you feed quarter after quarter into the machines. After twenty minutes without a hit at one machine, you move on to another. You notice someone sits down at the machine you just left, pulls the arm once, and an endless stream of quarters starts pouring into the tray. *Bummer*, you think to yourself as you drop another quarter into "Cleopatra's Treasure."

These situations should get you thinking about how much influence you believe you have over what happens to you.[1] They should also make you think about how prepared you are to respond to what happens, not just to avoid a bad outcome but to pave the way for a good one.

Here's something that's true: you can't always control everything that happens. The roller coaster will roll, the river will run, storms will rage, and the chips (or quarters) will fall where they want to fall. But here's something that's also true: you *can* control how you respond to these events. If your head is in the right place, you can be ready for what happens, eagerly poised to take on whatever comes your way. This is the **future-ready mindstate**.

Your mindstate is the perspective you have in any given moment that encompasses your current thoughts, feelings, and focus and determines how you experience the present. It perceptually and cognitively influences the choices you make about how you act or react. In the same way your pupils get bigger or smaller to adapt to the amount of light around you, your mindstate fluctuates based on the content and context of the moment.

In a future-ready mindstate, you're tuned up in these key dimensions: **optimism**, **openness**, **curiosity**, **experimentation**, and **empathy**, as well as your **Dimension X**.

Radical optimism goes far beyond seeing a glass that's half full. It reframes problems as positives and embraces a vision of an exceptional outcome. It enables you to see opportunity in every aspect of your experience.

Unreserved openness is free-falling into the (metaphorical) arms of others, not because you trust them to catch you but because you trust yourself to benefit from what happens whether they catch you or not. It puts you where opportunity can find you.

Compulsive curiosity turns you into a native in the land of the unknown. It gets you caught up in mystery and wonder exploring roads you've never taken. It creates pathways to opportunity that didn't exist before.

Perpetual experimentation fuels immediate discovery. It tests ideas rapidly and repeatedly and keeps pressing you toward where the learning leads. It determines the most desirable opportunity to pursue.

Expansive empathy connects one human experience to another. These are the intersections you create and the bridges you build on the path toward your future. It compounds the impact of every opportunity.

Dimension X is your unique superpower, the force that runs hot in you. It has a strong hand in what's happening to you right now as well as in what your future will look like tomorrow. It sparks you to act on the opportunity.

These are the dimensions of your mindstate that help you align your talents and character with your aspirations for the future. What makes them so powerful is that in combination and fully amplified, they form a way of looking at the world that reveals potential all around you. They influence the choices you make more than other factors, in part because they come from the most deeply human place inside you.

They need to be exercised, however, to develop the "muscle memory" that gives them their power. When these dimensions are not engaged, your best choices aren't visible or accessible to you, and other elements of your nature (such as fear or anxiety) drive your choices, landing you in places you aren't always happy to find yourself.

But when you hone these dimensions, extraordinary things happen. For one thing, you can't wait for your future; you're excited about where your choices may take you. You also make many more choices, and more choices means more opportunity. You are always moving forward—these dimensions will never pin you down or pull you backward. Finally, they make your future immediate and concrete, not distant and abstract.

Understand that the dimensions of a future-ready mindstate are not a framework. They don't represent a turnkey, structured approach to your future. They are dynamic, independent but complementary factors that fluctuate and are continuously emerging, unfolding, and recombining. People are attracted to frameworks and static models because they put ideas into a familiar context. But the real world isn't like that. I don't want you to cling to something familiar in these dimensions. I want you to see something new and to relate to your future differently as a result of engaging each of these dimensions.

These dimensions are also not all engaged simultaneously or to the same degree. They complement one another, to be sure, but there's no delicate algorithm that draws them out in a comprehensive or coordinated way. Every experience wants its own future-ready response—sometimes it will call for more openness, other times more empathy. Like the DJ mixing tracks, dialing up the bass for one song or tweaking the tempo of another, you learn to be sensitive to which dimension to tap into in a given moment.

Where Is Your Future-Ready Mindstate Today?

Consider this situation:

You have dreamed of being a doctor since you were a kid. You graduated from a good medical school and are in your third year of residency at a top teaching hospital. You knew the path you'd chosen wouldn't be easy, but the grueling hours, sleep deprivation, and lack of collegiality among your peers is making you seriously contemplate dropping out of your program. You're looking at $200,000 of medical school debt, however, and you have no idea what you would do for a living if you don't become a physician. You never expected to find yourself in this position. Should you drop or stay?

Circle the statement under each dimension below that best represents what you would be thinking as you're having this important talk with yourself.

Radical optimism	Unreserved openness	Compulsive curiosity	Perpetual experimentation	Expansive empathy
I will easily find a more rewarding career.	I'm eager to discover what's possible.	What can I learn from my experience?	I know how to figure out what's right for me.	If I don't love this profession it would hurt my patients.
I may feel better about my situation later.	I'm not sure what else I could do.	What if there's more to medicine than being a doctor?	I wouldn't know where to start to identify a new career.	My peers may also feel this way.
It's too late to switch gears now.	Medicine is all I know.	Maybe there's nothing new for me to learn.	I don't want to choose the wrong new career and fail again.	I need to take care of my own security and obligations.

Now draw a line connecting your circled statements under each dimension. Most people will see a kind of wave that shows an elevation for some dimensions and a dip for others. After a rewarding day at work or a solid night's sleep, you might even choose different statements and see a different pattern when you connect them again.

Just engaging in this exercise puts your head in an interesting place, doesn't it? Your mindstate is fluid, continuously adapting to context. And these dimensions are humming to varying degrees within your mindstate. You might have a high degree of optimism but not be curious enough to discover what else is out there. Or you may be open to a different experience but not be experimental enough to identify the best next steps. Even though you've spent almost eight years and buckets of money on this journey, maybe you're not ready to make the choices necessary to have the future you really want.

You're familiar with "fight, flight, or freeze"—those default stress responses that kick in when you suddenly feel threatened. These are automatic reactions you can't control that are determined by your nature and previous experiences. Your mindstate is distinct from these responses. Your mindstate can influence your behavior and decisions, even in the face of the same event that's causing your fight, flight, or freeze response. For example, the optimistic or open aspects of your mindstate might quickly take you beyond the stress response and turn the moment from a threat into an opportunity.

Imagine you're visiting Asia for the first time—first stop, Tokyo. You're taking a bullet train to Kyoto for a day trip. Just as you arrive, you realize you can't find your cell phone. You madly search your pockets and backpack but it's not there. Did you leave it at the hotel or lose it in the taxi? Should you turn around and go back to Tokyo to deal with this now? You're not thinking clearly because you're having the classic "I lost my cell phone!" panic attack. You take a beat to talk yourself out of doing anything rash, and after a couple of minutes, you decide you're not leaving without seeing this city you've researched for months.

What now? You hop on the subway and get off at Fushimi, which is the name of a Shinto shrine you remember reading about. Instead of finding the shrine, though, you realize you've ended up in the Fushimi sake district, where you spend hours soaking up the five-hundred-year history of sake brewing in Kyoto. On the train back to Tokyo, your brain is buzzing with ideas about how this ancient industry is innovating and adapting to make a place for itself in the future.

You see how these dimensions can have a long-term and immediate influence on your choices. They already exist inside you and can be cranked up at your will. They can also be cultivated and strengthened to become another kind of default response, one that ensures you're ready to make the most of whatever comes your way.

Now let's consider how the engines of creativity and imagination light fire under the dimensions of the future-ready mindstate.

Creativity, Clarified

In my experience, creativity is mostly misunderstood. It's held up as a rare strain of genius bestowed by the gods on the lucky few. That's mostly because people are dazzled by the "what" of creativity—the work of art, the disruptive technology, the scientific breakthrough—not the "how."[2] We're so impressed by the creative act that we promptly put it out of our own reach—I could never do that! We become spectators instead of actors, waiting for someone else to create the next amazing thing instead of creating the amazing thing ourselves.

I began considering the role the creative process plays in future readiness after I started working with the Stanford d.school in 2009. There I was exposed to an approach to design that made me see design as a verb, an active process that combines convergent and divergent reasoning to identify problems or opportunities and develop new ideas and solutions. Soon I saw the creative process as the more important component of creativity.

Focusing on the creative *process* instead of the creative *product* helps break down that false perception of creativity. The creative process is simply the way your brain makes associations across everything your senses take in. Everyone makes these connections constantly, sometimes consciously, sometimes unconsciously. But they're happening all the time. What you do with those connections—that's the crux of the relationship between creativity and future readiness.

As much as we can't take our eyes off of the sparkly output of creativity, in fact, the heart of the creative process is the input, which I think of as dots—lots and lots of dots. These dots are the countless pieces of information, experience, and ideas that are all around me at any given moment. When I'm receiving creative input, I'm seeing these dots. I'm alert to their presence. I'm also collecting the dots. I'm gathering some of them and introducing them to my thoughts. The optimism, openness, and curiosity of my mindstate enables me to see the dots and collect the dots.

Now the creative output starts. I begin connecting the dots, playing with the infinite combinations that the information and ideas can form. As a result of these connections, sometimes I push something new out into the world. My empathy, openness, and experimentation enable me to connect the dots.

You control creative input by sensitizing yourself to the existence of the dots all around you. You can train yourself to see more dots and bring them closer to you. You control creative output by choosing to do something with the dots. You can train yourself to connect more dots and make something new with them.

How many dots could you possibly encounter on your commute to work every day? You walk the same five blocks to the subway station, ride the train for exactly eight stops, get off, and walk three more blocks to your office, stopping at the coffee cart at the corner before heading inside. When you're on autopilot, you don't see much of anything. Or I should say you see the same old thing, which by now is invisible to you. Open your eyes and you'll see plenty.

If you make a point of looking at every person you pass on your walk to the station, or getting off the subway one stop earlier, or buying your coffee someplace new, by the time you sit down at your desk, you will have slightly different thoughts and ideas rolling around in your head than usual. Nothing groundbreaking, just different. The creative stimulation—the dots—you invite into your head today may help you solve a little problem that nagged at you yesterday.

Creativity is a multidimensional construct that is expressed and manifested in different ways—some tangible, some intangible. As we dig into a deeper understanding of the dimensions, you'll see how creativity feeds growth in each of these areas and helps you cultivate the raw material of which your future is made.

Imagination, Reimagined

The futurists love a good visual. Whatever trend or prediction they're promoting usually comes with a vivid picture of how it will make the future look different. We also have Isaac Asimov, George Lucas, and—let's be honest—the Jetsons to thank for a lot of the compelling images we associate with the future. Does imagining these far-off futures help you get ready to meet them when they arrive? Not much. But imagining the future that's right in front of you does.

To imagine is to set aside what's "real" or "true" right now to consider alternatives and consequences that are not readily apparent. The futurists imagine in order to develop predictions of the future, while designers imagine a range of scenarios that represent certain possibilities of the future. The future-ready person imagines their path to the future—specifically, the choices they might make that comprise their next step forward.

Thinking about what you're doing now and imagining what you might be doing differently just an hour or a day or a week from now—what I call "keeping the future close"—gives you immediate power to influence your future. This isn't outcome-oriented thinking; it's an incremental process that asks you to use your imagination to see just beyond what's ahead. As a result, your imagination helps to create these interesting opportunities for you to make intentional but risk-taking choices. In a sense, you kind of need to go out on a limb so that you can imagine the very next possibility.

How might you use your imagination to keep the future close? Say you have always yearned to publish a novel. By day, you toil away at your job, but at night you dream of seeing your story beaming back at you from a bookstore shelf. When you think about your novel, you see it happening far in the future, when you have the time and resources to devote to writing. You also safely place all those daunting obstacles you will face when you're finished writing your novel—finding an agent or a publisher—in the distant future.

Then something jarring happens in your life—a job change, a family crisis, a global pandemic—that turns your priorities upside down. Your novel is no longer an empty shoebox marked FUTURE that sits on the top shelf of your closet. Suddenly you can clearly imagine an immediate action—something you can do right now—that might make a book actually happen. You begin to set aside time early in the morning to write a couple hundred words a day. A few months later, when you've got a whole chapter under your belt, you find a writing partner to give you feedback that keeps you motivated. As your novel takes shape, you join an online writers' group that helps you understand the publishing process. Now you can see three or four very clear steps ahead of you that may get your manuscript in the hands of a publisher.

Are you holding a book in your hands yet? No, but you pulled the future close to you and imagined the small, achievable steps you took to write a novel. That future is becoming real—no longer a day-dream. Along the way, you may have discovered possibilities beyond publishing a novel, possibilities you would never have encountered when you held the future off in the distance.

Your imagination is not just focused on the future, but also on the past and the present. You consider all manner of artifacts—literature, art, or architecture—to conjure an image of some moment in history. Your own experiences, memories, and emotions combine with your five senses to feed your perception of the present. When you turn your attention to your future, you draw on all of those resources to imagine what should happen next.

One of my last projects at Google was called Project Reimagine, an organization-wide initiative launched in the early months of the pandemic with the intention to develop a next-gen, flexible/hybrid workplace model for the company's 135,000 employees worldwide—a six-week innovation sprint I led to literally reimagine how we would like to work in the future. I asked twenty-five leaders from across the organization to share metaphors that described what the workplace might look like in three to five years—say, a beehive or a space station. But thinking that abstractly and that far ahead was a challenge for them, as it was for all of us during that time; most seemed only able to focus on the immediate material needs for a work-from-home setup that would allow Googlers to continue to do their jobs every day.

In the 1990s, Google basically invented the future of work—from developing nontraditional campuses and workspaces to promoting activities focused on personal well-being, even to upending the con-cept of a dress code ("Just wear something" is the company policy). Yet now, with the door to the future of work pushed wide open by the pandemic, the organization found itself unable to seize this opportu-nity to shape the next new way of thinking about work. During this period of exceptional uncertainty, they drew a blank when I asked them to imagine something just a few years off.

One of the reasons we get stuck in the present is because we accept the constructs in our lives as fixed, words and images among them. But the vocabulary of the present is usually insufficient to describe and realize your future. Your imagination can provide you with a new vocabulary—words and visual or physical artifacts—that describes your future as you shape it. This continuous visioning informs each step you take beyond the present.

Here's an example: You use the word "career" to describe the educational and occupational path taken over a lifetime of work. So your career = school and jobs. What if today you decided instead to use words and images oriented around your life experiences or learning to describe your career? Maybe the segments of your career are called "episodes" that encompass the many aspects of your life, not just your employment. Maybe the episodes are associated with shapes or colors instead of chronology. Ultimately, this would probably change what the term "career choices" means to you, and your résumé would look less like a ladder and more like who you are and what you value.

Your imagination is an immediate, intimate tool that's essential to the day-to-day shaping of your future. Whereas practicing creativity nurtures the dimensions of a future-ready mindstate, practicing imagination allows you to recognize and describe your future as you use the dimensions to craft it. Both get stronger and more impactful with practice and lead to increased, better, and more diverse choices.

The biggest risk you take in an uncertain and ambiguous world is to walk backward into the future, extrapolating from the past and assuming that what was true yesterday will be true tomorrow. At the same time, just casting your searching gaze into the distant future is to miss the live wire of opportunity that's right in front of you.

The future is something that you must make for yourself. You actively shape your future through your choices, choices that reveal themselves through the practice of creativity and imagination and are acted on through the dimensions of your future-ready mindstate. When you truly understand all of the choices that are possible for you (think of Neo in *The Matrix*, when the code becomes visible to him), you will realize how much power you have to influence your future.

You may never guess correctly about what will happen in the future, but you can always be ready for it. Invest in developing your future-ready mindstate and you will be equipped to make the interesting, proactive choices that represent a future you've crafted— YOUR future.

Do you
believe
you
can

SHAPE

your

fu-

ture?

Try This

Make a square frame with your fingers.

Look through this frame panning to
the left then to the right.

Look above you. Now look down. Zoom in
and out.

Do you see something different(ly)?

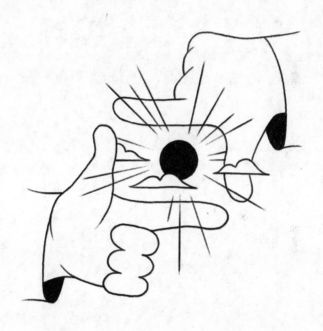

CHAPTER 2

Radical Optimism

Radical optimism goes far beyond seeing a glass that's half full. It reframes problems as opportunities and embraces a vision of an exceptional outcome. You absolutely believe something better comes from every experience.

Consider the simple equations below:

$$5+3=8 \quad 4+6=10 \quad 2+4=7 \quad 9-3=6$$

If your first thought was, *Hey, one of these equations is wrong*, you're not alone. (And you're correct, of course.) Our brains are wired to recognize mistakes first. This "negativity bias" evolved in humans to help us survive. We learned to look for bad or wrong things to avoid danger. Our built-in attraction/aversion to errors and faulty outcomes may have protected us from extinction over the course of human history, but it also taught us to cling to what we know right now instead of being open to the unknown, possibly dangerous future.

Here's what this negativity bias looks like in our daily lives:

That suitcase you've dragged around since college finally gave out, and you've spent a couple of hours looking around online for a new one. You've found a good deal on a great brand and model, so this should be easy . . . except you can't stop scrolling through the ratings on the company's website. There are dozens and dozens of big thumbs-ups from happy customers, but your eye keeps landing on the few cranky complaints. It doesn't matter that the negative reviews are mostly about shipping snafus and not the quality of the product. They are lodged in your head, and you end up clicking away despite all your research pointing to this suitcase being just right for you. That's the negativity bias.

Anyone who has lived or worked in New York City knows the cardinal rule when riding the subway: Do not make eye contact. It's a corollary to the unwritten rule most of us follow when we encounter strangers. Our default is to keep to ourselves when walking down the street or sitting on an airplane, so that we're less likely to expose ourselves to other people's problems or pain. We anticipate the negative possibilities and avoid contact, even though that stranger might actually end up being a lifelong friend or a romantic partner or the source of ideas or information that could change our lives.

Or this: You've arranged to meet a new business prospect at a conference in Denver. When you sit down to dinner, the initial small talk focuses on a problem with the hotel room or the flight delay that pushed back the meeting an hour—not the restaurant's stunning view of the Rocky Mountains, not the sophisticated menu you'd heard so much about. It's that one thing that didn't work out that gets the attention, especially when it comes to travel, when we're already feeling a little disoriented and untethered from our usual routines.

You can understand how negativity bias tends to control your day-to-day narrative. Research has shown that it takes at least three positive emotional impressions to counter every negative impression you experience. How is it that optimists manage to avoid this constant battle against negativity we're hardly aware we're waging all the time in our heads?

Optimists believe in and expect positive outcomes. Optimists picture the potential of a good outcome and put all their chips down on it because they have a kind of transcendent confidence ("My hike on Saturday will be great! Who said anything about rain?").

Does a person's belief that good things will happen actually make them happen? No, but optimists have confidence in their ability to effect change, which makes them more likely to take action and realize their positive vision. Also, the optimist's positive frame of mind makes them see good things where others might not. This alone—spending more time focusing on good stuff than bad stuff— explains why optimists tend to be healthier, live longer, and exhibit more resilience in the face of adversity than their pessimistic counter-parts.[1]

The future-ready mindstate calls for a more pointed and purpose-ful positivity, a way of seeing the world that I call "radical optimism."

Radical optimism is a belief in the potential not for good or for perfect, but for "better."

My work in the area of innovation allows me to spend a good deal of time in the realm of better. I have seen extraordinary breakthroughs born of a person's absolute certainty that there's something better to be attained—a better technology, a better product, a better service, a better process or protocol, even a better human being. They may not know exactly what that better will be, but they believe that over time, their efforts will produce desirable outcomes.

What innovators know is that better is the result of constant, persistent iteration. They tweak and test and tweak and test some more to improve on what's in front of them. The best innovators are not trying to hit the ball out of the park—they're looking for the smallest degrees of better that will move their work to the next level and then the next.

The pursuit of better is about progress, not perfection. Achieving the best is rare—there are only so many GOATs in the world. But when you orient yourself around better, every day is filled with infinite and immediate opportunities to succeed. The radical optimist chooses to seize these opportunities, creating a rhythm of iteration that hums on multiple levels throughout their day-to-day lives.

Google Glass was one of the most exciting projects I've been a part of. Developed by the Google X "moonshot" research lab, the smart glasses went through thousands of iterations as they progressed from idea to prototype to product. With every sprint, the team gathered countless pieces of information that they documented each week in three categories: technological, social, and design. We tested a lot of ideas about how someone might interact with the device. For example, those cool multitouch interfaces that Tom Cruise feverishly manipulates in *Minority Report*? It turns out they make your arms really tired, really quickly. We also briefly prototyped an idea using another device to record the user's conversations throughout the day, except we discovered that users actually had no interest in reliving the mostly trivial dialogue they engage in every day.

On a daily—even hourly—basis, the more we tried, the more "better" we achieved.

When an early version of the product was put in the hands of eight thousand beta testers under the Glass Explorer program, the feedback these users provided blew up a number of the developers' assumptions. Ultimately, Google Glass didn't turn out to be the next big consumer tech hit many people expected it to be, although the Glass technology contributed to important advancements in multiple areas—health care, journalism, hospitality, and emergency services, to name a few. But everyone I knew on the project showed up every day filled with this exuberant confidence that they would advance learning, whatever the fate of the product. The experience showed me in the most remarkable way how radical optimism's focus on "better" fuels progress.

I've noticed something weird, though. Even while humans tend to fixate on "the best," we also have a tendency to settle for "not bad" or even "good enough" in ways that not only ensure that nothing will improve, but eventually lead to decline. Take our relationship with gasoline. For decades we've been comfortable with the costs (both financial and ecological) we've paid for our dependence on fossil fuels. Until recently, most people have largely chosen not to focus on what could be better about their dependence on gas. Enter a global pandemic, a fluctuating economy, a war in an oil-producing region, and a host of other contributing factors, and suddenly every time we fill up the tank, we're paying more—by far—than ever before in history—and the environmental costs of our settling for the status quo have become inescapable. Think for a moment about all the incremental things we could have been doing all these years to be in a better place than we are right now.

The radical optimist isn't willing to push "better" to some far-off point in time. We believe that better is possible in the very next moment. We understand that we're choosing better and behaving in ways that achieve better right now. This provides instant gratification and the motivation to keep choosing better over and over again until it's who we are—someone who sees the future as the better place we are creating for ourselves.

Being a radical optimist both grounds and elevates your expectations. You're a clear-eyed realist—you can see there's a mountain in front of you. But you are confident that there's better on the other side of that mountain and there's no question you're going to make your way to whatever that unknown potential may be.

How do you train that inner lens to see the potential for better? How do you transform challenges into the opportunities that pave a path toward your future? Two critical approaches that help you to cultivate radical optimism are: saying the right kind of "yes" and creating a different frame of reference.

Just Say Yes

You're running a meeting and someone shares a new idea. It sounds off point and impractical. Your first thought is to shut it down to keep the meeting focused on the matters at hand. That's part of your job, isn't it, making sure your team accomplishes its assigned tasks? If you said no to the idea, it's likely no one would object or even notice because they're so accustomed to being herded inside the lines. (It's also likely the meeting would end on time.) But what would happen if you said yes?

First, let's consider what would happen to *you* when you say yes. It takes your brain off autopilot and immediately causes you to engage. Instead of just running the meeting, you're a part of whatever comes next. You're going to listen and reason more actively and look for the benefit that may result.

Now what happens to the other people in the meeting? You flipped a switch and the group dynamic visibly shifts. People start to light up; body language changes. They are suddenly as engaged as you are simply because yes is in the room. They are more inclined to see possibility and creatively address obstacles. The group is energized and excited to see an idea begin to take shape.

Who knows if all this will lead to anything? The most important result of saying yes is igniting the potential of the moment, seeing something happen that wasn't planned or otherwise calculated. This experience ever-so-slightly changes everyone involved by getting them thinking about what might be or what could be. It might embolden one person to offer a spectacular new idea at a future meeting, it might cause someone else to tackle a personal problem differently, and it might well make you rethink how your meetings should work. Consider how Isabelle Schnellbüegel, Chief Strategy Officer of Ogilvy Germany (and former Googler) incorporates "yes" into her work.

Learning to be Certain About Uncertainty
ISABELLE SCHNELLBÜEGEL

I lived through a trauma quite early in life that told me that I can survive almost anything.

It gave me a resilience that has shaped my life philosophy to put myself in positions that make me a little uncomfortable or afraid. Because I know that I will survive those situations, I push myself and take things head-on, which invariably has led to personal growth and opportunities I would otherwise not have encountered.

There's a kind of "say yes to everything" in me that changes the dynamic when I'm working with teams or in trainings and workshops. Especially when my rational mind is telling me, "That idea is no good," I push forward with "yes, and . . ." to provoke creativity in myself and within a group. This tends to help break down expectations related to people's roles in an organization— you know, that only certain people in certain roles can come up with ideas.

Even in a creative agency like Ogilvy, you can see some fear on people's faces when this happens . . . maybe they're worried about their status if the intern or the finance guy offers the best idea or solution. They may also be concerned about violating an established process they have for ideating or problem-solving. So it can be uncomfortable for them initially, but over and over again I have seen them come to this phenomenal realization that the group has reached a better result by accepting any and all ideas, wherever they come from. From a business perspective, this process has bridged the gap between the strategic and creative functions in a powerful way.

Ultimately, this is just enabling diversity of thought, which is a basic best practice, right? Personally, I get my best ideas from conversations with people who come from completely different fields than my own. Talking to people who are very different from me kind of excites and inspires me. I always learn something from them, but I also benefit from their unique perspectives, which help me tilt whatever I'm considering at that time and see it another way.

I go into every new experience with a certainty that I will gain something from it. It's not that I think that it's just going to magically work out. Well, maybe there is a little magic in it, but there's also a lot of effort. I believe that radical optimism is sharing that certainty that I have with others, bringing them along on what I know will be a path to something better.

The simple act of saying yes begins to break down the negative bias that constrains your own thinking and behavior. When you say yes instead of no (or you say yes instead of saying nothing), you can set all kinds of exciting variables in motion. If the language of no is your native tongue, how do you become the person who says yes?

Early in my career, I spent a lot of time in Japan, where I observed a curiously wonderful behavior in many of the friends I made there. Often when I asked a question or extended an invitation, my Japanese colleagues managed to respond with a "hai" (yes) even when their answer was actually "no." I might invite a friend to my home for dinner on Saturday night and they would say something like, "Yes, of course, dinner at your home would be very special! The following Saturday would be a great time to get together." See the trick there?

No "no," so I don't feel rejected or disappointed and everyone is happy that they will see each other one Saturday soon.

At the next opportunity when you want to say no to someone, slow down the conversation until you can find a way to shift your response to make it a yes. Say you're running late for a meeting and you bump into a colleague you haven't seen in a while. They ask you to have a quick cup of coffee to catch up. Turn "No, I'm late for a meeting" into some kind of genuine yes. Observe what happens to that person when you do this. You will see that they feel appreciated and respected. Pay attention to what happens to you, too. Not having to put on your "no" armor leaves you more relaxed and comfortable with your own behavior. Spending this little extra effort is satisfying to you and the other person—and the immediate outcome is just the same as if you'd said no.

Googler Newton Cheng likes to ask the question "What would have to be true?" He poses this scenario: "Say we need to build one thousand fitness centers next year. Most of my team would rightly say it can't be done. But if I say instead, 'What would need to be true to build one thousand fitness centers next year?' we would go through an innately optimistic thought exercise and find a way forward."

Most often we say no out of some kind of fear. We were social-ized from a young age to protect ourselves by saying no. Next time you are about to offer the usual negative response, ask yourself what you might regret not experiencing if you say no. For example, you've been invited to a professional networking event, the kind you mildly dread and purposely avoid. After a long day of work, why would you want to spend another two hours talking about more work-related stuff? To protect yourself from boredom, fatigue, and shaking hands with strangers, you say no to the invitation. But what if your future business partner is at the event? Or you never hear about that book that could change your life from the person getting coffee next to you? Or you don't meet those two guys who love craft beer as much as you do?

Change Your Mindstate: Premortem

You may have been a part of project postmortems, those meetings where you and your colleagues evaluate what went wrong. A premortem asks you to imagine what might go wrong so you can prepare for potential mitigation strategies. You can also use a premortem approach to consider what might happen if you choose not to act.

When you're thinking about turning down an invitation of any kind, ask yourself the questions below:

What might happen at the event that I would regret having missed? Imagine someone is describing this event to you after it happened. Make a list of incidents or conversations that you would have enjoyed or benefited from had you attended.

What might not happen at the event because I didn't attend? Make a list of incidents or conversations that weren't possible because you weren't there.

What could happen thirty or ninety days from now that would make me sorry that I didn't attend this event? Looking ahead to future impact, make a list of the opportunities that might not present themselves to you because you skipped this event.

This experiment is not meant to trigger FOMO. It's just going to make you think harder about what happens when you choose no.

You also have to learn to say yes to yourself. This is the simplest and most powerful bit of self-talk there is. Say it out loud in the bathroom mirror every day. The more often you say yes to yourself in private, the easier it will be to actually say it in public when you have the chance.

Finally, look for the next opportunity to say yes to someone else. Think of a person you tend to shut down with no. The salesclerk who's trying to upsell you. The colleague who's always inviting you to lunch. The neighbor who's asking you to volunteer for a street cleanup. Next time, say yes and notice how it makes you feel. There will be an immediate sense of letting go because you're no longer controlling the outcome by saying no. Instead of tensing up, your physical response softens as your body prepares to go for a ride. You're also more attentive and sensorily engaged. Do this a few times and you'll notice how you perceive ideas that are presented to you in a more flexible and creative way.

Full disclosure: saying yes is time- and resource-consuming. I guarantee the meeting I had you running a couple of pages ago was fully subsumed by that new idea you said yes to. Which means that all the other items on your agenda didn't get accomplished.

It might help sometimes to think of yes as signifying affirmation, not agreement. It's similar to a "like" or thumbs-up on social media. "I hear what you're saying and appreciate that you're saying it." "I recognize that you have a point of view that I may not entirely align with, and I'm okay with that."

I will also point out that you have to get used to being down with wherever yes might take you. Sometimes when you say yes, things get messy or even go wrong altogether. But this teaches you that you don't need to control where things go. And it teaches you to accept an imperfect outcome and—like a Japanese kintsugi artist—find a way to transform it into something new, something better.

Every time you say yes, you get a little better at opening a box, knowing that anything at all could be inside. It's a snake! It's a sweet potato pie! It's a jar of rubber bands! After a while, it doesn't matter what's inside because you just get used to that "whatever it is, just bring it" feeling. Let's put it this way: When you go to the airport planning to take a flight to New York, saying yes might put you in Singapore by the time it's all over. Buckle up!

Yes, But . . . ?

I'm taking a moment here to note that "yes" isn't a magic wand that changes the world. Specifically, I'm thinking about the way we often say "yes" as if we're poised to open a door, but then follow "yes" with "but" and slam it shut. "Yes, but . . ." and "no" are the same. They're both excuses for why something isn't possible, which isn't where you want your head to be in terms of your relationship to the future.

Try to remember the last time you used "but" in a sentence. Now write that sentence down. Maybe you're thinking, *I would like to write that sentence down, but I don't have a pen or paper handy*. And here you are, stuck by choice with just an excuse to not do something.

Now let's revise that sentence and replace "but" with "and": *I would like to write that sentence down, and I don't have a pen or paper handy*. Do you see the opportunity? Swapping "and" with "but" points you to what to do next. Let's try a few more.

I would like to get more physically and mentally fit, but I don't have much time.

I would like to get more physically and mentally fit, and I don't have much time.

I would like to spend more time with friends and family, but my work keeps getting in the way.

I would like to spend more time with friends and family, and my work keeps getting in the way.

"But" is literally a stop sign. It gives you permission not to proceed. "And" eliminates the excuse and puts a hot light on what you could or should be doing. Try to catch yourself next time you say "but" and replace it with "and." See how it reveals the excuse you've been making to yourself?

Now Say "Yes, And . . ."

Just saying yes immediately removes barriers for yourself and others, which on its own is an exceptional outcome. Saying "yes, and . . ." sets things in motion.

"Yes, and . . ." has its roots as an exercise in improv theater,[2] where a person makes a statement ("I remember when we went to Mexico") and the next person builds on that statement ("Yes, and there were ferocious thunderstorms every afternoon"), followed by the next person ("Yes, and the sun would come out again just in time for happy hour"), and around the room until a whole world of detail has taken shape around the original statement.

Early on at Google, I taught the art of building ideas. I created a full-day workshop called Improv for Innovation that I used to train thousands of people around the globe to shift their thinking away from their own preconceived ideas and create something new by "playing" with each other's ideas. I introduced "yes, and . . ." to show them how to start with something—anything, really—and see where it might go. The exercise immediately created the space and opportunity to allow ideas to develop.

Without fail, "yes, and" caused the people I trained—small teams, large groups, and individuals ranging from project managers to engineers and designers to CEOs—to end up in a different place than they anticipated. I often started the training with this prompt: *Think about your team's next off-site meeting.* In the first round, I would ask someone to offer an idea and I'd instruct everyone else to offer their "good" reasons why it was a bad idea. Once someone started by saying, "Let's go on a cruise for our off-site." Cruise ships are crowded and noisy. All the activities on a cruise ship would be distracting. Cruise ships are environmentally objectionable.

Next, I asked everyone to switch their position to supporting the cruise ship idea with "yes, and . . ." "Yes, and let's invite our families or friends to join us on the cruise. Yes, and let's open the agenda to our families and friends. Yes, and let's include creative challenges in the agenda that we need to solve as teams. Yes, and let's focus the challenge on ways to balance the impact the cruise has on the environment." We are all so good at coming up with a list of "why nots." The next time someone starts listing all the reasons an idea won't work, ask them to name the one reason (or more) it might work. This particular exercise led to an actual waterborne class I later taught called "The Entrepreneurship."

Over the course of the training, I could see people's eyes widen as they realized what they were creating together—a concrete, actionable idea that hadn't previously existed. They would write to me later to say that the experience had been exhilarating and had changed them. They would describe how they took "yes, and . . ." back to their work and transformed their approach to collaboration and interacting with colleagues. Best of all, they would tell me about the new ideas that came out of "yes, and . . ." and how gratifying it was to bring others into such a rewarding process.

"Yes, and . . ." is the radically optimistic response because it doesn't just welcome a "crazy" idea, it picks up a hammer and helps build it.

Google's Street View technology got its start in 2001 in a lab at Stanford, where a couple of researchers were considering a way to combine videos to create static pictures (there's an idea). Larry Page had been thinking about whether it was possible to photographically map the whole planet (yes, and . . .). He was interested in testing their concept and camera prototype, so he mounted the camera on his car to capture video as he tooled around the streets of San Francisco.

Before long, a handful of Googlers who had heard about the idea offered to use their 20 percent time (Google's policy that gives every employee one day a week to work on projects outside the scope of their job) on this project. They wanted to see if they could expand on it by adding a spatial recognition component to the technology (yes, and . . .). The resulting 3D-ishness of the photography and the project's capacity for data collection brought more Googlers and their ideas out of the woodwork (yes, and . . .), and by the end of 2005, Street View became a "real thing," a project approved by Google leadership (yes, and . . .) to see where it might go.

As a result of hundreds of "yes, and . . ."s that advanced both the technology and its multitude of applications, Street View contributed to the development of Google Maps, Google Earth, and Google Arts & Culture, to name just a few groundbreaking initiatives. Sitting on your couch at home, you can tour the world's great museums or World Heritage sites, explore the ocean floor, or see a satellite image of the street where you grew up. Did Larry get his map of the world? Not yet, but thousands of volunteers have worn backpack-mounted Street View cameras to photograph some of the most remote places on the planet. The top of the world isn't a bad place to end up.[3]

"Yes, and . . ." instantly creates a dynamic that is generative and constructive—it's like a big bucket of Legos for building ideas. Put it to use in a variety of situations. Got a logistical problem? "Yes, and . . ." might reveal that you actually have a supply problem. Having trouble making a decision? "Yes, and . . ." may lead you to even better options than you have been considering. Trying to settle an argument at the dinner table? "Yes, and . . ." can turn the conversation from a squabble into an unexpected level of understanding. When you're building toward solutions using "yes, and . . . ," you encounter discovery, opportunity, and always a better problem.

Use "yes, and . . ." to let go of "me." In our personal and professional lives, many of us care about being in control and often say no to give weight to our own opinion. "Yes, and . . ." puts a bit of distance between your brain and your ego and allows you to hear other perspectives with objectivity and openness. "Yes, and . . ." can liberate you when you find yourself in the grip of your own point of view. Instead of continuing to press what you think, use "yes, and . . ." to throw open the door to others' unexpected ideas.

In organizations, "Yes, and . . ." inspires a culture of generosity and confidence, a place where ideas can grow because people feel supported and believe that their contributions are valued. At the Stanford d.school, one of our standing class principles is "make other people shine." In your personal and professional interactions, "yes, and . . ." makes you feel looser, less afraid of making mistakes, and more naturally collaborative. Ultimately, "yes, and . . ." allows you to explore options that are out there even if you can't see them yet—in other words, it can carry you toward your future.

Change Your Mindstate: Robot

Certain activities are tough to do working closely with another person—moving furniture and navigating a road trip immediately come to mind. This simple exercise shows what happens when you use "yes, and . . ." to work with someone—in this case, to design a robot.

Find a collaborator, a piece of paper for each person, and one pen. For the first round, Person #1 draws a line on their paper to begin creating a robot. They hand the pen to Person #2, who draws a line on their paper to begin creating a robot, then passes the pen back to Person #1. Person #1 adds a line to their drawing, then hands the pen back to Person #2 to add another line to their drawing. After fifteen or so back-and-forths, there should be some kind of robot on each piece of paper.

Compare both robots, choose the one you prefer, and discard the other. On the blank side of the paper you've kept, start the process over again, this time passing the paper and pen back and forth to build the robot together, stroke by stroke. After another fifteen or so exchanges, stop and compare the robot on the back of the paper with the robot you created together. Which do you like more? Probably the one you drew together. Why? Because when you accept someone else's idea and build on it (yes, and . . .), you're both invested in making it better.

Reframe

Saying "yes" and "yes, and . . ." limbers up your brain to see the potential for better. The second approach to developing radical optimism—reframing—helps you see something altogether new.

We tend to review the events of our lives through a frame that is based on our beliefs, biases, and experience. It's in our human nature to try to make sense of the world and we use this frame to do that. The frame develops over the early years of our lives, and while events later can certainly alter the frame, it tends to be pretty much baked by the time we're making the big life choices about relationships, careers, where we want to live, and what we want to do with our time. The frame influences those big decisions, but also all the millions of little decisions we make every day, right down to what we wear or eat or literally what next step to take.

I went on a six-day hike in the High Sierra in California with three friends. We covered a daily distance of about a half marathon, usually at an elevation of eleven thousand feet or more. (To appreciate the rest of this story, you probably want to know that I have a hard-core fear of heights.) On day two, we were crossing the Kings-Kern Divide on Lucy's Foot Pass, a very steep, Class 2 pass with short Class 3 and Class 4 sections and a deserved reputation for dangerously loose talus. We made it to the top but quickly realized that we had taken an off-trail route that brought us to a five-hundred-foot vertical drop that seriously limited our options for getting out.

Aware of my issue with heights, one of my friends encouraged me to focus just on each rock where my hand and foot would go. With one grab, one step, one grab, one step, I made my way across the pass. Zooming in so closely to the immediate moment—just what my body was doing and what I was feeling—allowed me to move forward without fear. Sometimes the objective is simply to move forward, one foot in front of the other, to get to a place where you can adjust your perspective and take in more information.

After that hike, exhausted and grateful, I made a point of zooming out to appreciate the vastness of this mountain range, forged over millions of years, and to which my presence was just the tiniest blink of an eye. Each day I am one grab, one step forward toward the future I'm making.

Reframing isn't about changing who you are, it's about changing what you see (the focus) and how you perceive what you see (obstacle or opportunity). The thing itself isn't changing either. You are changing your relationship to the thing by looking at it differently.

Let's start with what you're looking at. When your focus is narrow or close, you operate with blind spots. Hey, what I can't see won't hurt me, right? Maybe, but what you can't see may also be something tremendously beneficial to you that you'll never know was *right there*. Changing the aperture—zooming out—lets you see other aspects of a situation. It provides context that helps you understand the systems and relationships around whatever you're looking at and ultimately helps you make better decisions based on your more informed understanding.

Nothing will teach you how (and why) to zoom out better than Charles and Ray Eames's *Powers of Ten* design film.[4] Starting with an overhead view of a couple having a picnic in a park, in a span of about nine minutes, the film zooms out every ten seconds until you're looking at Earth from one hundred million light-years away, then it zooms back in even faster until it's focused on a skin cell of one of the picnickers. This little "adventure in magnitudes" demonstrates that perspective is everything, and more importantly, that perspective is entirely within your power to control.

Say a work situation has been nagging at you. Your team is having trouble collaborating to complete a project. You've met with each of them, and they're all performing their roles exactly as they should. You take another look at the project itself. All on its own, it seems to make sense, but there's definitely something about it that's confounding the team. You zoom out a little to try to understand whether this project syncs with the services and deliverables your team is expected to provide. You zoom out a little more to see how the project fits in the overall business strategy. Something about this view catches your attention, and you zoom back into the project requirements and realize that the project's problem statement is off. In other words, your team has been using all the right tools to solve the wrong problem.

Zooming out and in can actually help you sleep better at night. I'm serious. Next time you're lying awake fretting over a personal problem—maybe you're in a rocky patch with a close friend—practice zooming out. Right now, all you can think about is the last testy exchange you had with your friend. Zoom out and think about your friendship over time, how your friend has been a constant source of support and good humor when you needed it most. Think about how often your encouragement has made a difference in your friend's life. Zoom out a little more to remind yourself of what your lives looked like before you were friends. When you zoom back in, you might realize that you're both just growing and looking for ways to express your changing needs. So this problem you're losing sleep over may actually be a healthy, productive thing you're going through and not a problem at all.

Focusing on the upside of a downside situation lets you see possibilities nested in problems. This positive reframing isn't a denial of a negative event, it's just an acknowledgment that there is more to the outcome and experience than only the negative. In the positive frame, you can see the "better" you can take away from a difficult experience.

Reframing is how you'll see the potential and opportunities inherent in any problem. Here's a way to think about it: Take a piece of paper and draw a vertical line down the middle. On the left side, write "Problems" at the top and list all of the problems—big or small—that you're currently facing. Pose each problem as a statement.

On top of the right side, write "Possibilities." For each problem you've listed, tip it and tilt it and look at it sideways and upside down until you see the opportunity for better. Pose each possibility as a question.

Problems	Possibilities
Working from home is driving me crazy.	How might I work from anywhere and feel calmer, more productive, and more creative?
I live in a place experiencing drought, extreme temperatures, and water shortages.	What lifestyle choices can I make that don't contribute to the climate crisis?
Customers aren't coming to my store anymore.	How can I serve my customers where they are?
I feel stuck in an unpleasant family dynamic.	Where can I find the emotional and social engagement I need?

Keep playing with this reframing exercise and you'll recognize a few things. First, you'll see how much power you tend to give to your problems. Second, you'll see how little effort, if any, you normally spend trying to identify the potential for better in the circumstances of your life. Finally, you'll see that considering the possibilities associated with your problems ignites optimism and creativity in equal measure.

Sometimes reframing is just a matter of taking a problem and making it a better problem. I call this "climbing the right mountain." I once worked with the global elevator and escalator manufacturing company KONE as their innovation consultant. (You may not have heard of KONE, but you have likely been transported on one of their products.) I spent time with teams in the United States, Finland, Italy, Mexico, China, and India, teaching them to apply a user-centered, prototype-driven process to solve complex problems.

We would start by looking at an age-old challenge in the elevator world: users think the elevator is too slow. I asked them to describe KONE's usual options to address this problem. They might install a new lift mechanism, replace the motor, maybe recalibrate the timing algorithm. Next I asked them to reframe the problem to focus on what's really bothering the consumer: the wait is aggravating and boring. Now they could think about the problem in a variety of creative ways—install mirrors or play music or videos. They could even provide hand sanitizer—killing germs also kills time, you know.

Every time they practiced reframing a problem, they recognized an opportunity to do something better, something special. Lightbulbs were going off over every head—they were discovering things they hadn't thought about creatively in years. We reframed challenges including managing people flow in one-hundred-thousand-plus-person buildings, mitigating the risk of falling into a shaft, and ensuring people's physical safety in an elevator cab. The experience was so remarkable that the company went on to establish KONE

Innovation Labs to cultivate new champions to scale innovation to more individuals and teams around the world.

Generally, the bigger the problem, the bigger the opportunity to reframe and make it a better problem. Thinking about who you're creating a solution for, place your challenge inside a "How might we . . ." question. Consider this: When I take my kids for ice cream, they never fail to make a mess of themselves and most of the back seat of my car with their dripping cones. I have a problem!

How might we create a new kind of cone for eating ice cream without dripping? Putting a solution in the question (a new kind of cone) doesn't allow you to come up with various ways of solving the problem or may even cause you to misidentify the problem.

How might we redesign dessert for everyone? This is way too broad and it's not a problem that needs solving.

How might we redesign the ice-cream-eating experience to be less messy but still fun and portable for small children? This is a problem for our specific audience (the sticky kids in the back of my car) that can be solved.

You get a better problem when you ask yourself why you want to solve the problem, as this enables you to reframe it to be more meaningful and practical. When you ask yourself how you'd solve the problem, it lets you reframe it to be more specific, actionable, and achievable.

Another effective way to reframe is to avoid assigning so much weight to certain circumstances. I remind myself all the time that nothing is permanent and so there's no benefit in my becoming too attached or involved in what's happening because it's bound to develop into something else entirely or may even just disappear.

I often begin talks about future readiness by asking people to write a description or draw a picture of what they imagine when they think of the future. I usually notice some anxiety in the room as people wonder whether I mean the drones-and-flying-cars kind of future or just, you know, the what-might-happen-tomorrow kind of future. They seem really invested in getting the "right" answer.

Later in the talk, I ask them to crumple up the paper with their idea of the future and throw it on the ground, which many are visibly resistant to doing. My point? Attachment is the enemy of innovation. You have to let go of the need to have the right answer and change your relationship with the answer itself. Just spending a couple of minutes sketching an idea causes this audience to become emotionally attached to it—they like their idea, they are prepared to defend it, and they can't think of any other idea but the one they're holding in their hand.

To get to your next better idea, you have to detach from your current idea. Meditation practices teach this so powerfully, to observe your thought or sensation then gently and kindly let go of it to make room for something new. Practicing this situational objectivity is the radical optimist's secret weapon when things feel especially fraught—we know things will shift and are certain that better is just a moment (or a breath) ahead of us. Former Googler Kalle Ryan is especially adept at letting go in order to segue to the next opportunity.

Setting the Stage for Magic

KALLE RYAN

I'm Irish and Swedish, raised in Ireland by parents who valued creative expression maybe more than anything else. As an adult, I lived in New York City for seven years, fully immersed in the creative life. I played music, I wrote poetry, I performed in front of audiences all the time. When I moved back to Ireland, all that stuff was bubbling in me, and I was like, "I gotta do some shows." I was disappointed when I couldn't find anything like what I'd been doing in New York, then I realized I should just make the gig I would want to go to. I picked a theme and invited some artists from different disciplines and put them in front of one another. I ended up doing this gig for ten years, it was called the Brown Bread Mixtape.

I'll never forget this moment: It was just the second or third show, and I was leading the audience in a sing-along—I think the song was "My Blood Is Boiling for Ireland."[5] The space was heaving, and it felt like electrical wires were crackling across the room. It was just a bunch of people bellowing my silly song, but in that instant there was joy on every face and I felt this perfect sense of fulfillment. We were all hungry for the same thing, to feel creatively connected. It was everything.

For a long time, while I was working for Google and later Meta, I joked that my corporate self was Bruce Wayne and my creative self was Batman. For someone in whom the creative impulse is so strong, I knew that the stark line I drew between work me and creative me wasn't right or even healthy. One day I asked myself,

What if Batman came to work? Okay! I answered right off, *and what now?*

From this point on, I saw my work in a completely different light. I started asking, *What is the creative way to look at this? What is the creative way to understand this? What is the creative way to articulate this?* Where previously I solved things the way that was expected, now I see creative opportunity in every task or project in front of me. You want to do a musical version of your presentation slides? Oh, yeah, we're definitely trying that. If it crashes and burns, what's the worst that can happen? It didn't work, but we learned something today that we didn't know yesterday. I'm down with that any day of the week.

Changing this frame dramatically altered the trajectory of my career. I forged a very distinctive approach to internal organizational communication while I was at Google that was very visual and utilized a variety of media. Turns out Batman was just what this very corporate function needed.

No matter how much you try to mix things up or keep yourself off-balance, you're going to find you're on a traditional path from time to time, and when you do, you realize that you've built up a lot of risk aversion. I push through this by saying to myself, *I can't risk not taking a risk.*

My radical optimism is kind of a trust—not knowing what I'm going to get when I land but trusting that whatever it is will work. I'm excited and terrified, but I know I'm going somewhere new. You have to trust that the magic is out there ahead of you and be ready to do something with it when you get there.

In 2016, I partnered with the United Nations to help the global institution grow an innovation culture. Over the period of four years, I conducted trainings with staff, managers, and executive leadership in Turin, Italy; Geneva, Switzerland; and Madrid, Spain, to develop a corps of ambassadors to accelerate innovation across the organization. A good number of the people I met from agencies including UNESCO, WHO, IMF, WIPO, and UNOCHA described the UN as slow, hierarchical, and change averse—all true, perhaps, but still just excuses for avoiding the risk and experimentation necessary to find new solutions to the massive problems it is the UN's mission to tackle.

My focus was to help them get past the excuses and become an organization that could generate ideas they could get excited about. The soil was hard when we started working together—it took effort to break it up and make it a more conducive environment for innovation. The organization had been doing this work so long they thought, *Hey, no one understands the problems we're dealing with better than we do.* When presented with the concept of reframing, however, they sat up with a jolt, realizing they weren't doing nearly enough to understand the specific needs of the people they served.

It took courage for the UN to admit that they were missing out on shaping the future and to do something about it. I saw exciting growth and learning during my time with them, and I was inspired by their radical optimism—they see the world as it really is, but they also see a world that can be better.

Radical optimism is all about better. It believes in better. It wants to sample and remix and riff on ideas to get to better now. It wants to be the Sherpa on the path to opportunity. Can you find your future without radical optimism? Sure, if you don't mind stumbling around in the dark, grabbing at anything, reacting to everything. Radical optimism is a light that reveals the potential your future represents.

Do you

SEE

opport

the

unity

all
around
you?

Try This

You return home from the supermarket and discover that a bag of someone else's groceries has been mixed up with yours.

Look at the next page and rotate the book to consider four ways things might go.

Where might each of these paths take you?

You call the store and are told to keep the groceries. You empty the bag and discover a box of chocolate cake mix and birthday candles.

You drive back to the store right away to return the groceries, but the owner of the bag isn't there.

You call the store and are told that the owner of the groceries can be found in the coffee shop across the street.

You drive back to the store right away to return the groceries. You get into a minor car accident in the grocery store parking lot.

CHAPTER 3

Unreserved Openness

Unreserved openness is free-falling into the (metaphorical) arms of others not because you trust them to catch you but because you trust yourself to benefit from what happens whether they catch you or not. You accept the dare to expand your perspective.

After I finished high school and did my year of civil service in Germany supporting patients who have Alzheimer's disease and delivering food to elderly people, it was time to take the next step. I was interested in being a chef, but I was scared to leave the safety of my home and community, so I applied for jobs at restaurants close to home. Fortunately for me, nobody offered me a job, and I had no choice but to step outside of my cocoon to figure out what would come next for me.

I took a ferry across a lake not far from my town that borders Austria, Switzerland, and Germany to study at the University of Konstanz. While my journey was similar to any other young person headed off to college, it was a big leap for me. I was shy and unsure of my purpose, and I didn't have much confidence that I would find community there or even succeed as a student. My vague intention was to study technology and education, maybe psychology and design. But the profound learning I experienced there had less to do with my studies and more to do with the transformation of my own belief system. Over time, I realized I had been kind of holed up inside this fortress of assumptions about my educational, emotional, and material needs that didn't really serve me well. I suppose I could have tackled them one by one, weighing and testing and adopting a new set of values. But somehow I knew I was facing the most important opportunity of my life—to fully open myself to ideas and experiences I had not yet encountered and find out for myself what I believed, where I fit, and how I could have impact in the world.

This was the start of the unreserved openness that I've pursued ever since. The pure state of giving yourself over is the key to having confidence even when you're uncertain or uncomfortable. Openness almost always starts with a leap. You behave as if you're open to it— you dare yourself to jump—then discover after taking the leap that it actually caused you to be more open the next time you have a chance to leap. Openness is generative—that is, a little bit generates more openness, which generates even more openness, and so forth. Every time you choose to jump, you reinforce your openness. The more you choose to close yourself off, the more you deny yourself. It really is as simple as that.

All of us are closed to some extent. The status quo bias tends to close our minds to anything that threatens our current situation. Personal habits, traditions, and social norms are the armor of a closed mind. They give us permission to avoid doing something else or something new. And whenever we happen to crack open the closed door to a new experience, we pat ourselves on the back for our courage and adventurousness, then quietly shut the door again and go back to the regular rhythms of our lives.

Being closed wrongly signals that you think you already know everything you need to know. Why should I try that new idea when my old idea works just fine? Trust me, opportunity doesn't find you if you cling to just what you know now. Instead, it limits your capacity to learn from new experiences and ensures that your interests will remain static and narrow.[1]

Besides depriving you of countless opportunities, being closed stiffens you against change. And given that change is happening *all the time*, this puts you in a permanent defensive state. Think of a clenched fist—that is both physically and mentally exhausting. Of course you're tired; you're fighting a law of nature—impermanence!

An interesting thing about openness is that it turns off and on like a spigot, open one minute and closed the next. To become more conscious of these choices you make, register your response to one thing that comes at you during the course of one day—anything that pops up in your day and prompts a reaction from you.

Say a college friend is calling to ask you for a favor. Or your boss wants you to revise that presentation deck again. Or the person outside the grocery store is hustling you for spare change. What might the open response be in these instances? How about the closed response? And what might the outcome of these different responses be?

Considering your own experience, first you'll notice that the open response is less stressful than the closed response would be. Being closed and resistant takes more out of you physically and emotionally than being open and willing to listen. The open response is also more positive because you're looking at what's possible instead of what's impossible, which contributes to your sense of well-being in the moment and beyond.[2] Finally, the positive response is more promising because you're triggering creativity and collaboration rather than conflict.

When you find yourself going straight for a closed response—falling back on your standard perceptions, preferences, or habits—shake it off by taking a moment to focus on one sensory thing—the color of the sky, the smell of a freshly cut lawn, the sound of morning traffic. Think of words that describe the object of your focus. This will snap you back into the present and flip the open switch.

Let's admit it: we crave certainty. Most of us will opt for the sure thing over the not-so-sure thing because of the tension and anxiety we feel being in a state of uncertainty. Yet it's the people who pick the not-so-sure thing and choose to be open to whatever might happen that make the future look different from the past.

A compelling, electric feeling comes with unreserved openness—a heightened awareness, the kind of productive nervousness a performer or athlete feels, with a buzzy confidence in their ability to react to the variables they know they will encounter. They're accustomed to that feeling because it's intrinsic to what they do. The rest of us have to work intentionally to detach ourselves from routines and invite different stimuli into our lives to find that slightly off-balance, on-your-toes sensation of being open. This moves you out of your comfort zone and into a zone of learning and growth where anything can happen.

One day in December 2017, I was walking into my classroom studio before a lecture when I got a call on my cell phone from a German number I didn't recognize. I had a few free minutes, so I answered the call. It was Oliver Bierhoff, the German football hero who scored the "golden goal"[3] in the 1996 European championship to secure victory for the German national team. I have to admit that I'm not a big football fan, but I was pretty sure this would be an interesting call.

He had read an interview I did with *Der Spiegel* titled *"Yeah, lasst es uns versuchen*" ("yeah, let's give it a try") about how to build an open, innovative, and forward-thinking culture and had tracked me down to see if I would meet with him. As director of national teams and football development for the German Football Federation (Deutscher Fußball-Bund or DFB), Oliver was looking to bring German football back to the World Cup–worthy performances that had won them championships in the past. He was convinced that the organization needed to open itself to a new way of doing business, and he was looking for inspiration outside of the world of sports—hence, his call to me.

The DFB is the governing body of the entire German football league system as well as the men's and women's national teams. As a result, the organization has a tremendous influence on the culture of the sport in Germany, from the most elite level of professional play down to the local youth football being played in just about every town in the country.

You can understand why I would jump at the opportunity to train innovation coaches from among the top management, players, and referees of all the professional football clubs in the federation. I was eager to see not just how these leaders might apply the concepts I had been testing at Google and Stanford's design school, but also how a new way of thinking might impact the larger, 6.8-million-member federation.

In interviews with Oliver and other DFB members, I learned that the organization was stuck in an outdated frame of mind. When they looked in the mirror they saw the champs they used to be. When they tried to picture the future, all they could see was the past. As a result, the DFB had become bureaucratic and self-absorbed, more focused on preserving what they were than on finding out what they could be. I wanted to help them let go of what they used to know and make their way to a different future.

I hosted a workshop for DFB about futures thinking and innovation culture at Google's office in Hamburg; then, over a period of several months, I worked with them at their headquarters in Frank-furt. The DFB was trying to build a culture where people were eager to solve old problems in new ways, so we developed rituals for the organization and the teams to support being open to new thought patterns, innovative ideas, and a healthy feedback culture.

Athletes and other sports professionals are famous for using rituals as psychological touchstones, so I had a hunch that this ap-proach would resonate with this group. I frequently tap the power of rituals in my training because they're so effective in breaking down routine thinking and behavior and making way for fresh perspectives. Too often, an organization's values are just flat, aspirational words on a website or in an employee handbook. Rituals can be powerful tools for bringing those values to life.

To encourage openness and experimentation, DFB designed rituals associated with these values. A sharing ritual called "eigentor" or "own goal" was established where one teammate describes a poor decision or failure and the negative consequences that re-sulted, then the rest of the team helps to identify what can be learned from it. Another ritual, called "neunzig minuten" (ninety minutes—the amount of time a regulation football match takes), was created to give everyone in the organization an opportunity to focus on their work without interruption from 10:00 a.m. to 11:30 a.m. every day. The Lunch Lottery was introduced to bring people together from different parts of the organization. Two employees are randomly paired up for five lunch dates at which they're encouraged to "learn something different" from the other person. Special guests occa-sionally make an appearance (Lothar Matthäus! Birgit Prinz! Manuel Neuer!) and "#lunchselfies" are widely shared. They have discovered that these rituals they've created produce unique moments, little catalysts for meaningful growth and change.

Oliver Bierhoff saw the potential to create a culture of openness and reimagine how the DFB functioned as an organization, as well as how it approached training teams and players to build a winning dynamic for the future. You may be wondering, *But* are *they winning again?* The women's national team came *this close* to taking the 2022 UEFA Women's Championship, losing to England 2–1 in overtime, so yes, things are looking up. The more important result, however, is the more holistic, values-oriented way the organization sees itself, as evidenced by the DFB's new headquarters on thirty-seven acres in Frankfurt am Main. The campus was specifically designed to encourage informal meetings and to make it easy for employees and visitors to view the outdoor activities from any building, so that the business side and the sport side could learn and flourish together.

Consider how Adam Leonard, executive coach and Googler, used meditation practices to encourage tough-minded engineers to become more open to uncertainty.

Opting for Open

ADAM LEONARD

Like most young kids, I asked a lot of questions and the adults in my life always seemed to have the answers. Naturally, I assumed that adults had everything figured out. One day I asked my mom a particularly tricky question and she gave a surprising response: "Nobody knows that yet. It's a mystery." I had never heard the word "mystery" before and felt exhilarated to learn that some questions don't yet have definitive answers. A new motivation arose within me. I not only wanted to learn what's already known, but also to explore the unknown.

My thirst for new discovery—that feeling of awe and wonder about what we don't know—has followed me into my adult life. I see openness as a primary means of discovery. But it takes courage to remain open in the face of mystery and to venture outside one's comfort zone into unknown territory. It's much easier to retreat back to the common and familiar. The journey from the familiar to the unfamiliar usually feels uncomfortable. So, when I'm at the brink of an unknown, the trick is to practice being comfortable with being uncomfortable.

Travel has been a good example of this for me. I'm a big proponent of what I call "improv backpacking," just traveling somewhere completely new without a set plan. When I travel this way, I trust that I will discover new people to meet, new sites to see, and new places to stay that I couldn't have known about beforehand. Not having a preconceived agenda can feel both scary and freeing at the same time. It opens the possibility for more spontaneity and coincidence. For me, tons of creative energy gets generated from all the freshness and unpredictability that comes with visiting foreign places in this way. I've done this kind of multimonth backpacking several times in my life, and each trip has been transformative in different ways.

I've applied that same sense of openness to traveling inside myself as well. When I practice various forms of inquiry, contemplation, and reflection, I never quite know what I will encounter. Whenever I investigate within, I aim to stay open to what I might find—to notice rather than judge. These inner journeys regularly lead to unexpected creative insights that enhance my life.

My first 20 percent project at Google was "gPause," an initiative intended to introduce mindfulness and meditation to different corners of the organization. Bill Duane was Google's Head of Wellness at the time and the company's now-famous Search Inside Yourself program was in full swing, training growing numbers of Googlers in meditation and emotional intelligence. I had practiced meditation for many years before I joined Google, and I was happy to see that his trainings were popular. But I noticed that the meditation rooms around the campus weren't really being utilized, so it was hard to tell if people were transitioning from training to actually practicing. So I decided to establish a practice community to encourage some unlikely adopters to give meditation a try.

I thought about how I could inspire a bunch of really smart, analytic engineers to take up something so strange to their culture as meditation. Well, I knew these folks had a love affair with the scientific method, with experimentation in particular. I decided to talk to them about meditation in a scientific way. I proposed the hypothesis that meditation had numerous benefits based on many neuroscience studies. But they could only confirm or disconfirm this hypothesis by running the experiment on themselves, treating their own mind and body as the laboratory and collecting data from their direct, first-person experiences. "If you want to be a good scientist," I said, "you have to run the experiment."

For a whole lot of Googlers, this has been the key to opening their minds to a seemingly weird practice that they discovered could be very useful and rewarding in their lives. Since the launch of this one community of engineers in 2016, daily communities of practice formed in over 160 Google offices across the world. All that calm focus, restorative energy, and creative insight spread across the globe, stemming from thousands of individuals choosing to open themselves to something new.

Much of my core work focuses on helping leaders have deeper and more meaningful conversations to address the most complex challenges they face. The technology industry often gets excited about new and improved platforms for communication. And I do, too. But I get even more excited about the quality and conscious-ness of a human-to-human conversation, regardless of the medium.

The best leaders I work with practice what I call "evolutionary dialogue." This practice involves a balance between confidence and humility—the confidence to express a point of view and humility to admit its inherent limitations. Participants open up to each other's perspective, get their egos out of the way, and hold the possibility that their minds might be changed (and even upgraded) through the dialogue. At its best, evolutionary dialogue brings forth a collective intelligence that's smarter and more creative than any of the individual participants by themselves. This way of relating typically doesn't happen by accident. It's a conscious choice that requires openness and vulnerability.

Science continues to investigate how human beings learn, grow, and evolve. We certainly don't have all the answers yet. But we do know that development tends to stall with a closed or fixed mindset. In contrast, an open or growth mindset allows us to step into our "zone of proximal development"—the sweet spot that's just beyond our current capabilities, but not too far beyond that we feel overwhelmed. That's where new possibilities and potentials emerge. That's where the magic happens.

Unreserved openness is a wide and welcoming embrace of life's ambiguity and uncertainty. Being open will take you to the really interesting, incredibly rewarding places you wouldn't otherwise find. In fact, those places are mileposts on the road to the future you're shaping for yourself.

How can you make sure you get—and stay—on that open road? By cranking up transparency, trust, and generosity, and finding new voices to listen to.

Try Transparency

Sometimes when people talk about being open, they're actually talking about being transparent. In interpersonal relationships, transparency implies we're laying it all out there—no secrets, no surprises. In an organization, it tends to mean that communication is frequent and direct and that operational information is readily accessible at all levels.

Unreserved openness is distinct from transparency, but they play so well together when you get it right. Think of openness as acceptance of what's coming in and transparency as acceptance of what's going out. Say you receive a bit of bad news. Openness lets you take it in, process it, do something meaningful with it. Now let's say you have to convey a bit of bad news. Transparency lets you share it honestly and without hesitation.

How do openness and transparency work together? One of my first and most memorable experiences occurred when I started working for Google in 2010: attending the weekly TGIF (Thank Google It's Friday) all-hands meeting, an in-person and virtual gathering of employees from around the world. Every Friday afternoon, Google's cofounders, Sergey and Larry, would say a few words and then open the floor to whatever employees had on their minds. Week after week, watching them take direct, sometimes uncomfortable questions and offer equally direct, honest answers was a master class in culture building.

Once an employee asked why Googlers weren't allowed to fly business class on work trips. Then-CFO Patrick Pichette responded that it was company policy for employees to fly economy class. He noted that he himself flew economy and felt it was fair to ask other employees to do the same. The conversation was lively and resulted in the development of a system called "trips" that allowed Googlers to accrue points every time they flew economy class or stayed in a less expensive hotel for work. When they had enough points, they could fly business class or first class if they preferred.

From the earliest days of the company, the founders used this social ritual to make the value of transparency real. Every Friday, I saw them use openness to grow their ability to roll with whatever happened—they never knew what they would face in these meetings—and use transparency to build trust.

Like openness, transparency is just a choice. Do I allow myself to be vulnerable by acting openly and speaking directly? Or do I protect myself by obscuring my behavior and keeping some (or all) of my truth to myself?

Also like openness, transparency is not always an easy choice. Being transparent invites criticism from people who might not like or appreciate what you're saying or doing. Why would you put yourself out there if you know you're likely to get burned? Well, for one thing, it's the world's best way to establish and maintain a trusting relationship.

Unfortunately, there's no such thing as "sort of transparent"— you have to go all in or not at all.

Being transparent takes a little getting used to. You can start by inviting someone else to be transparent with you. Request someone's unvarnished feedback on something that matters a lot to you. Find out what your kid thinks about a recent parenting call you made. Or maybe ask someone you supervise to give you a performance review on a meeting you ran. Switching up the communication-power dynamic and putting yourself in the listening seat can teach you a lot about how to be transparent yourself.

Another way to practice transparency is to be the first person to do or say the hard thing. For example, share a mistake that you've made. In our leadership meetings at Google, each person would describe something they had clearly gotten wrong during the previous week—maybe a poor business decision or a conversation that was mishandled. At first, it was uncomfortable to share these stories, mostly out of fear of being thought less of by our peers. But over time, trust was established and transparency became something that we expected from and valued in each other.

You could also share something you're working on that's not fully baked. At Google's TGIF meetings, one or two teams might share a very early stage prototype or demo of a new technology they're working on. Considering the audience, these teams would have good reason to be nervous. But I saw some amazing new collaborations and partnerships come out of those meetings. When teams risked testing their ideas (often incomplete) with a neutral, engaged, and critical audience, they actually increased the likelihood that their project would succeed because it attracted other smart people to their work.

My final plug for transparency relates to authenticity. So many of us only show certain sides of ourselves, not wanting to expose our flaws or insecurities. But when you communicate openly—without shades or filters—people know they're seeing the real you. This often prompts them to let down their guard and allow *you* to see the real *them*. Some of the strongest, most lasting relationships are born out of sharing our authentic selves.

To show who you are, the most modest gestures can have a big impact. I have an introverted friend who uses transparency in social situations that are difficult for him. Instead of standing alone in the corner at a party (or avoiding the party altogether), he introduces himself to someone and after a couple of minutes, he tells them that he's shy and parties aren't easy for him. Sharing this small truth establishes a bit of intimacy with the other person, who always seems to know what to say next. Many terrific conversations have followed, conversations that my friend otherwise would never have had.

Ultimately, being transparent is about showing our humanity. I'm not saying it's easy to do, but I am saying it's worth it. Try transparency and watch what it does to your sense of openness.

Change Your Mindstate: Clear

At Stanford University's d.school, our classrooms and teaching studios are what we call "empty by default." Most types of items you associate with a teaching environment (chairs, desks, whiteboards, etc.) are moved out of the room at the end of class. This eliminates expectations and preconceived notions of what the next teaching and learning experience will be like. Before each class, the instructor sets up the room to support the learning and discovery they hope to enable that day.

What can you do to your physical environment or to your routine to create a "default to open"? Clearing your workspace at the end of the day doesn't make the problem you're tackling at work go away, but it could help you return to the work with fresh eyes tomorrow. Or what about your electronic devices? You know how sleep experts advise us to put them away at night? How about doing that in the morning? Instead of starting your day consuming content, sit with your waking thoughts for a few minutes instead. Try to avoid picking up a device until you're ready to shift into work mode. You'll find the time you gave your brain to gently acclimate to the day sets you up in an open mode, more accepting and curious about what the day will bring.

Trust Yourself

Choosing openness asks you to trust yourself to make something out of whatever happens, whether it's good or not so good. That, of course, is the hitch. When we're open to a new experience and it turns out great, we're like, "Weeee, I want to try that again!" But when it doesn't turn out well, we file that memory away and tap it later to protect ourselves from future missteps.

Young kids constantly find themselves in situations where they have no idea what they're going to do. They don't have much experience to fall back on, so they just wing it at school, at home, on the playground. Eventually they build a frame of reference that reminds them of what can happen when they react this way or that way. Every time they make a "mistake," an adult usually corrects them, and then they join the ranks of the rest of us who follow the rules and mores we learn over a lifetime.

Try to remember how that felt when you were a kid, having no sense of what you'd do when something unexpected or unfamiliar happened. (The movie *Home Alone* comes to mind.) On the one hand, it was a little terrifying, right? It was as if someone tossed you a hot potato and you had to figure out what to do with it—fast. On the other hand, it made childhood kind of exciting, didn't it? There was a thrill to it that made you more likely the next time to say, "Hey, over here, pass me that potato!" Whether those moments ended in triumph or disaster, they showed you what you were capable of.

Fast-forward to today and now you're hardwired to see the hot potato as a risk or a threat and to feel a spike of anxiety when it drops in your lap. Your first thought might be, *How can I make this thing go away?* Instead of rushing to remove your unease, consider getting comfortable with it as a normal part of your learning process.

How can you react more positively and productively when the unexpected happens? First acknowledge your initial response. Are you worried? Angry? Frustrated? Okay, noted. Now remind yourself you can't change what happened, you can only change your attitude toward what happened—see it in a different light and make something more of it.

Say you just found out there's a major leadership change in your organization. Last time this happened, two people in your department were let go and it took a year for things to settle down. Based on your previous experience, this news makes you anxious. Think about this event as if it's something you're holding in your hands. Examine every aspect of the event and write down a list of descriptive details about it. Keep adding to that list until you identify an opportunity that the change may present.

This exercise puts you in a much more objective frame of mind. By the time you're done, you're still holding a hot potato, but you have neutralized the lifetime of cached responses you carry around in your head and now can approach the event instead with an openness to what might happen next. Over time, this will teach you to trust your open self to turn these unexpected events into stepping-stones toward your future.

Being open isn't always a headlong rush into the unknown. It can also be a gentle acceptance of the many different facets of your own day-to-day experience. Think about how much time and energy you spend reacting to random incoming stimuli, mostly without noticing that you're doing it. You can't stop the stimuli from coming at you—imagine a swarm of midges—but you can shift into a kind of slo-mo to be able to recognize what they are.

For example, a neighbor kid is teaching herself to play the drums. Most afternoons, she pounds away in her garage, making it difficult for you to concentrate on your work. You've bought noise-canceling headphones and thought a lot about calling the kid's parents to beg for mercy. One day instead of tensing up when she starts playing, you stop what you're doing and just listen. She's repeating an exercise over and over, and after a while you notice the slightest change, maybe a smoother transition or a more confident stroke. You smile to yourself when you realize that you're hearing her master some small thing. Technically, it's the same "racket" you've heard day after day, but now this intimate observation makes you hear it in a different way.

There are countless moments like this in a day, each of them an opportunity to experiment with observation and acceptance. Doing this walks you back to a more natural state where you're less encumbered by your visceral responses and prejudices. When you're sitting quietly with one of those moments, you can really feel what it means to be open.

Sarah Brown, who is a global operations manager for Google in Singapore, has used this approach to openness to find peace in the midst of constant change.

Listening to Yourself

SARAH BROWN

I've been with Google since 2011, based in Mountain View until 2016 and in Singapore ever since. Over the years, I've worked on a number of initiatives focused on learning, leadership development, and community engagement. Beginning in early 2019, I was involved in several projects that got shut down due to reorganization or changing priorities. The pandemic added to the jumble, so for four years I was switching roles every three to six months. There was just a tremendous amount of change and turmoil happening in my work and life during this period, so much so that I ended up in the hospital. My digestive system had kind of turned upside down from stress, and it took me a year of working with holistic doctors and nutritionists to feel like myself again.

It's funny how you don't know you're in a "learning moment" until you come out the other end of something like this. The world is a really crazy place going through constant change over which we have absolutely no control. A colleague of mine always used to say, "Control the controllables," meaning focus on what you have the power to change. I didn't really understand that concept until I was taken out by this health crisis.

In fact, I think there's only one thing we can control: our response to our own experience. Prior to my illness, I had been doing things that were healthy, such as running, cycling, and weight lifting. While those things were great for my physical health, they weren't the right tools for me to manage my stress. What I needed more of were practices that put me in tune with myself and enabled me to better read, understand, and regulate my emotional state. Learning how to know myself and connect to my own somatic signals has altered how I respond to change and stressful situations. I have developed a deeper sense of my own strength and ability to cope in challenging moments, and a greater openness to cultivating the conditions I need so I can meet those moments successfully.

Being open requires a high level of trust in yourself and a degree of optimism for the future. You have to believe that whatever you need is out there in a way that enables you to relinquish the idea that you have to try to control things. Openness and control seem to me to be on opposite sides of a spectrum. The need for control suggests that we're afraid and don't believe that things will turn out in our favor. Openness coupled with optimism feels like a genuine sense of trust in the universe. It's the ability to say, "Well, this isn't what I thought I'd be doing or what I'd imagined for myself, but it could lead me somewhere interesting that I didn't expect."

Cultivating this optimistic openness in me has led to a greater sense of calm that essentially replaces much of the stress I would previously have felt. Whatever is going to happen is going to happen. When I face that fact with openness and curiosity and a sense of my own strength, it's exciting rather than scary or stressful. I try to reflect on each day and account for the difference this perspective shift makes in the way I approach my work and relationships. The exercise helps me identify patterns in my own narrative and points me to opportunities to make different choices or recognize when I'm making progress.

Due to another unforeseen shift in the Google organization, today I am in a role that I would never have chosen or sought for myself at this stage of my career. But instead of being frustrated or anxious at this turn of events, I see opportunities to learn and develop new skills. There are other professional experiences I hope to have, but I value where I am in the present. For my health and overall well-being, this has made all the difference in the world.

Be a Sharer

The open-source model for software development made some people nervous when it came on the scene in the late 1990s. It seemed crazy for one company to release original source code—for free—and allow other parties to modify or build on it to make a product of their own. In fact, the concept has been around for a long time and has probably done more to fuel innovation in the last hundred years than any other factor.

To toss such valuable intellectual property out into the universe like that, you have to have an enormous amount of faith that the benefit of sharing will be greater than the cost of sharing and be willing to put everything on the line to prove it. Take this kind of high-stakes sharing down to the personal level and you could really make yourself sweat!

You'll be comforted to know that I'm talking about sharing a couple of simple things, not billions of dollars' worth of proprietary code. That said, the kind of sharing that is characteristic of unreserved openness is just as purposeful—even as calculated—as it is for Linux. We share to enable future possibility and opportunity. Think of it as an investment with a big payoff down the road.

The act of sharing creates pathways to discovery. Each instance of sharing sets off a series of interactions and events that unfold in a multitude of directions. There's a kind of choose-your-own-adventure aspect to it, where one share leads to X and a different share leads to Y, each of them spinning off their own chain of results. The more you share, the more pathways there are to explore.

When you share, you put something out there but you also get something back. What you get back might not be apparent right away or even for a long time. In fact, the multiple waves of impact are continuously rolling out and rolling in again, each time washing over you with a different effect.

Because we live within a massive technological infrastructure built for sharing, I should note at this point that I'm not concerned about what sharing tools you use. I care only that you do share and about what you might share with others, starting with your ideas.

Sharing an idea is an act of trust. An idea is a delicate thing, like a sketch of something taking shape in your head that's still very personal to you. History is filled with stories of people whose ideas were mocked and misunderstood, so it's understandable that you feel protective and private about your own ideas. Here's the thing, though: an idea is a social creature. It needs to mix and mingle and make the rounds for you to find out if there's anything to it. Sure, it might get roughed up and break a little (or a lot), but it might also become something stronger because of what you learn from the sharing.

When you share an idea, you're opening yourself to the possibility of what it might or might not become. No more cogitating until the idea is perfect, now it's on the loose! Not long after I joined Google, I had an idea to create an innovation training center and community. Before I had a proposal or even a whole concept, I started to share this idea with folks from different parts of the company. From a professional perspective, it was a little dangerous to say my idea out loud at this point, knowing how easy it would be for people to poke holes in it or even sink it—I was still pretty new in my job, after all. But many of them got excited about it right away and their feedback helped me shape the idea that eventually became Google's renowned Creative Skills for Innovation program, or CSI:Lab for short, which we eventually shared with the world.

Sharing a human connection with someone is another powerful conduit to openness. Those brief moments when we relate to another person are so energizing and affirming, but how easy it is to forget to make these connections. How many times have you just hustled through your day, hardly looking up, barely noticing all the human beings you've encountered along the way?

Every time you open yourself to a purposeful, thoughtful interaction with another person, you increase the "dots" for personal connections—all of that creative input that's so important to your future-ready mindstate. Even the most fleeting contact can tip your thoughts or feelings in a different direction, causing a ripple that might bring together any number of internal and external touch-points of your day.

Sit down to lunch with someone at work whom you don't know very well. Talk to a stranger about the book they have in their hand. Say good morning to that person you see every day on the elevator or at the coffee shop or on the train to work. These moments of connection do two things: First, they force you to slow down and be human together with another person, however briefly. This is just something we need, like air and water and food. Second, they can provoke an insight or set something in motion that you might never have anticipated.

Once my wife, Angela, found herself standing next to a young police officer named Agnes while waiting in line at a local sandwich shop. When Angela ordered her sandwich, the officer noticed her accent and began speaking to her in German, which was a pleasant surprise. They talked for several minutes, and by the time they parted, they'd exchanged contact information.

Over the next year or so, Agnes became a part of our family circle. To our kids' delight, she occasionally stayed with them when Angela and I went out in the evening. (You'll never see such orderly and obedient children as those being looked after by a police officer.) Eventually she left Santa Cruz to take a job as a park ranger in Wyoming, but sometimes she emails and sends photos that remind us what an unexpected and positive presence she had been in our lives. I think of this often, how Angela's sharing this connection with a stranger affected our family during this time, in a way that may continue to influence each of us differently for years to come.

A final thought about sharing is a simple one: share your attention. Whether you're in a meeting with colleagues or having dinner with friends or engaged in a transaction with a salesclerk, just be all there. Any interaction will have more value to you (and the other person) if it has your full attention. When you divide your attention—by "multitasking" or looking at your cell phone or making that to-do list in your head—you contribute less, learn less, and feel less as a result of the exchange. You spent the same amount of time on it as you would have spent giving it your full attention, yet you have so much less to show for it. What's worse is how splintering your attention diminishes the potential of these interactions. Why bother having them if you're not fully open to what you can take away from them?

Take one day and try to give your full attention to every interaction you're involved in. You'll notice all kinds of details you might normally miss, from a facial expression to a particular word choice to a concern that's conveyed "between the lines" of the conversation. That's a lot of information right there—meaningful, even actionable, information you would not otherwise have. Sharing your attention may seem like it's on the liability side of the balance sheet because it takes time, but it's really on the asset side. I promise you will always gain more than it costs you to share your attention.

When you learn about sharing as a child, the grown-ups usually explain it as a kindness to others. By now you can see that the type of sharing I'm encouraging is for your own benefit. It nudges you toward an openness to engagement that creates shimmers of possibility.

Change Your Mindstate: Fly

Write a "what if" question about the future on a piece of paper. The question should be about something that matters to you personally or to your team or organization—something you think about a lot or aspire to. Fold the paper into an airplane,[4] tuck it in your bag or pocket, then go about your day.

Every time you feel the paper airplane in your pocket or see it in your bag, look around for someone nearby and imagine what would happen if you let it fly in their direction. Would they pick it up and read it? If so, how would it make you feel to share your dream or vision with a stranger? What if they saw the airplane but ignored it? Would you feel embarrassed or as if your thoughts don't matter? Sharing something of yourself without knowing how it will go over is an act of trust in yourself and in the potential to connect with others.

Seek Diversity

The business case for diversity in the workplace is ridiculously clear. A team composed of people who have different social and ethnic backgrounds and represent a variety of characteristics and experience bring differing perspectives to their work, which contributes to the group producing better ideas and more effective approaches to troubleshooting and problem-solving. That's a bottom-line-boosting boon for any organization that cultivates and supports a diverse workforce.

The same is true for each of us as individuals. When your personal ecosystem is diverse, your mind is more open to ideas and solutions that go beyond just what you know from your own narrow experience. The more you expose yourself to perspectives that are different from your own, the more possibility you will see ahead of you.

To build that diverse ecosystem for yourself, start by assessing what you've got going on right now. Who are the people you spend most of your time with? What do you read or listen to or watch? What kind of food do you like to eat? How do you spend your free time? Where do you go when you travel?

Take all this information and create a profile of yourself. Each aspect of your profile represents an opportunity to diversify. For instance, in the people category, do you spend your time with the same five people? Time to mix that up. Ask someone you know only slightly to meet for coffee. Volunteer at the library or a food pantry to be around lots of different people, all of them strangers. The idea is to spend time with people who are a) different from your usual crew and b) different from you.

In the innovation world, we look for new and interesting opportunities for innovation by engaging with "extreme users." These are the folks who are operating on the farthest edges of a challenge or a solution and can provide unique insights because of their particular perspective. For example, I have worked with teams focused on accessibility who engage with people who are blind and deaf to understand how they use technology in their everyday lives. This led to the development of the voice assistance technology that's known and used by so many of us today.

The opportunities to change your incoming stimuli are everywhere. Have you ever gotten in a rental car and found the radio tuned to a station that's not your usual fare? Don't touch that dial! Listen for a while just to get an ear for what's happening in that world. What about the books on your nightstand? Are they mostly mysteries or biographies? Maybe you're all up into science fiction. Just start slipping one title from another genre between the books in your favorite categories. Or add a book from another era or a book that's about a part of the world you know nothing about. Bring diversity to every corner of your life. Every area is ripe to welcome new influences.

When it comes to interactions with other people, being open to their perspectives starts with setting aside your own. The thoughts and ideas and opinions in your head are big and bright, like those giant digital billboards in Times Square. And they're loud! So loud it can be hard to hear what someone else is saying. We've all been there: the other person is speaking, but we're so busy watching for the chance to counter with our own position that we don't actually catch what they say. And we've been there plenty, haven't we?

Many of us were raised to believe that what we think is most important. We're taught in school how to express ourselves so we can be sure other people know exactly what we think. We're even told not to care what other people think, so as not to let it influence our own thinking or behavior—or to protect our feelings if they don't think much of us.

Actually, you should care a lot about what other people think. Why? Out of respect, for one reason. This is one of the most basic courtesies we can show another person, to demonstrate that we value their thoughts. It's part of the social give-and-take that lets us coexist together on this planet. You don't have to agree with what they think, you just need to believe that what they think matters.

You should also care to know what other people think because it strengthens your own thinking. Almost any exchange can broaden your own scope of understanding, either by confirming your thinking, challenging your thinking, or improving on your thinking. If you're not taking in any outside perspectives, you'll always be stuck with your own static thoughts.

Strive to be someone who welcomes another person's thoughts. Start by learning to quiet your own thoughts to create space for other people's thinking. For example, you might prepare for a meeting about a problem your team has been wrestling with by setting aside any preconceptions about what the solution might be and any expectations about what might happen in the meeting. Remind yourself to be open to wherever the conversation goes because you don't know yet what is or isn't possible. Ask simple questions and otherwise *just listen.*

Former Googler Raphael Tse applies this approach with a slight twist when coaching executives and teams. "I ask questions with no attachment to any outcome or solution. Staying in the open question space as long as possible gets you out of the 'shoulds' and makes room for more 'coulds.' It also tends to nudge people to shake off the stories they usually tell themselves, the default thinking that makes it hard for them to see other possibilities."

Another way to clear your head of your own point of view is to take the position that the other person is right and you're wrong, to assume that their idea is better than yours. The best time to do this is when you're 100 percent convinced that you're right. Stop the conversation and say, "Hey, I think you're on to something—tell me more." Giving the other person the floor, so to speak, gives you a chance to really hear them and recognize the potential in what they're saying.

You have to do this one for real. Don't just humor the other person by listening while you secretly still think you're right. Asking yourself honestly, "What if I'm wrong about this?" can help shoo away the certainty that's closing your mind to the other person's perspective. After a full and objective exploration of the subject, it may turn out you do have the best idea. But you'll never know for sure unless you genuinely open yourself to the possibility that you don't.

One of my favorite teaching exercises is what I call the "best worst ideas." The group is divided in half, and every person is given a green piece of paper and a red piece of paper. I ask them to describe in detail the worst restaurant idea they can think of on the red paper. Then I ask them to describe their best restaurant idea on the green paper. I collect all the papers and throw away the green papers with the best restaurant ideas. Then I distribute the red papers and ask them to take the very worst restaurant idea and turn it into a great one. They consider all the features of the bad idea and find a way to make it a good idea. The exercise forces them to let go of their attachment to their own ideas and rely on one another's thinking to come to a better conclusion. Some unusual concepts have come out of this exercise that have actually come true—what do you think about dining in the dark or ordering from an all-insect menu?

When you set aside the prejudice that you have in favor of your own perspective—in other words, you get out of your own way—to open yourself to others' perspectives, you'll see that they are as brilliantly varied as the wide world in which we live. An appreciation of diverse perspectives combined with a willingness to accept or try new things enables you to better navigate challenges and find novel solutions.

To be open doesn't mean you have to like or agree with everything you encounter. It just means you choose not to judge what's happening and instead just accept it and take it as it comes. Unreserved openness welcomes the good situations along with the bad, success as well as failure, because it's wholly focused on new learning and experience.

Every November on the Dia de los Muertos—the Day of the Dead—Google Xers gather all of their ideas that didn't work out—prototypes, project proposals, business plans, even Post-it notes—drop them in a coffin, then light it all on fire and celebrate together as these old ideas go up in smoke. They do this ritual together to put the past behind them and open themselves to what's next.

The late Zen master Shunryu said, "If your mind is empty, it is always ready for anything, it is open to everything. In the beginner's mind there are many possibilities, but in the expert's mind there are few." Be the beginner. Choose unreserved openness and you will discover the anything and everything he's talking about.

Does **oppor-tunity** find **you easily?**

Look just above the arrow on the next
page.

What do you see?

What do you think you know for sure
about what you see?

What don't you know at all about what
you see?

How can you find out more about what
you see?

CHAPTER 4

Compulsive Curiosity

Compulsive curiosity turns you into a native in the land of the unknown. It gets you caught up in mystery and wonder exploring paths you've never taken before. "What if" is your mantra.

When I was a kid, we had a set of reference books in our home called Meyers Enzyklopädisches Lexikon. I can't begin to count the number of hours I spent with my nose buried in those books, each organized alphabetically, bringing something that looked like order to the massive amount of information they contained. But this actually created a wonderful, occasionally shocking discordance to the experience, where I'd spend a rainy afternoon reading all about "*aalbeere*" (a currant-like berry) then turn the page and find "*aale*" (eel). It often felt like there wasn't room in my head for everything I found in those books. But that irresistible combination of fresh discovery and serendipity kept me coming back for more.

When you're young, you have no idea what you don't know yet. You're sent to school to learn what the adults think you should know, but there is—and there will always be—so much that those institutions could never show you. The extent to which you absorb or experience anything beyond that early prescribed learning is entirely dependent on your curiosity.

Take a moment and think about how many adults you know—including yourself—you would describe as curious. I mean deeply, actively curious. I'm betting it's just a couple of people, if any. Why is that? Studies show that the nearly 100 percent curiosity levels we experience in childhood plummet to almost zero by the time we're adults.[1] The more we learn as we grow up, the less interested we are in continuing to learn. It's not that we're no longer able to learn from new experiences, it's that we just don't care to. Other qualities, such as dependability, productivity, and resourcefulness, become more valuable to us, as they help to preserve the aspects of our lives that we've decided are most important.

It's true that children are naturally curious, but there's nothing childish about their curiosity. It's actually quite sophisticated. They make no assumptions about what they might discover. They are adept investigators, using all of their senses to gather information. They're comfortable being in a state of wonder—they don't need to have all the answers. At the same time, they ask questions *all the time*.[2]

I witnessed this firsthand when I traveled to the Galápagos Islands with my family. My kids were ages twelve, eight, and seven at the time. Our boat had barely anchored and they were already in the water, bobbing and diving among the sea lions, turtles, and sea stars. Over the next few days as we explored the islands, they absorbed complex information about the flora and fauna, the relationships between the species and their environment, and the spectacular balance of this delicate ecosystem. Learning that the tortoise's neck had elongated over centuries to be able to reach higher sources of food or how marine iguanas had more recently adapted to be able to swim in search of algae, each of them came to their own understanding of how all creatures—themselves included—adapt to ensure their survival.

My children's eagerness to explore was like a crazy hunger they couldn't satisfy. From the moment they opened their eyes in the morning until they dropped into a dead sleep at night, they were just driven to take in more. Each discovery made them bolder and more inquisitive. By the time we set sail for home, they were about to burst from the treasures inside their heads.

That's **compulsive curiosity**. Once engaged, it's the dimension of the future-ready mindstate that feeds itself. It's like the tickle of a feather at the back of your neck. A flicker of something out of the corner of your eye. The hint of an aroma wafting under your nose. They must be investigated! They must be understood!

It's kind of shocking how quickly we leave all that delicious curiosity behind. I've seen this happen with organizations time and time again. The most curious organization in the world is a start-up. It's got no money, no infrastructure, no institutional memory. What it does have is endless curiosity. What would happen if we did this? Why does A lead to B? How far can we take this? With more questions than answers, their curiosity literally propels them forward.

Yet even the most trailblazing, cutting-edge start-ups eventually lose their curiosity. They go from being voracious prowlers in the wild to bored idlers eating their lunch out of a vending machine. What happens to them? Just as their curiosity propels them into the realm of success, they are tamed by convention. They lose their unique perspective, their senses dull, they start to cling to what they have, and they stop asking good questions.

I was once asked by venture capital firm Sequoia Capital to speak to a group of twenty start-up founders, each of whom had a million dollars of Sequoia seed money in their pockets. They had been flown to London to participate in the kickoff of an initiative meant to provide training, mentorship, and development support to these fledgling entrepreneurs. During the day I spent with them, they were coached in telling their founder stories and articulating their vision for their start-ups. I talked to them about the future, specifically how to imagine the headlines about their work that they would want to see in the future.

I am a naturally hopeful person, but as I looked at these founders, their eyes sharp with intelligence and their cheeks flushed with excitement, I couldn't help wondering when the burning curiosity that got them to this point would flicker out. Like children, organizations grow up. They tend to lose the spark of curiosity that once defined them and wake up one day on an ordinary path, concerned about market share and stock options and board relations instead of the wonder of discovery.

It's at about this juncture when a mature organization comes to me to help them stimulate innovation. They're starting to feel some survival anxiety because they no longer feel in tune with their rapidly changing environment. They've forgotten how to probe and inquire and uncover information just for the sake of learning and understanding. And they spend all their time answering questions rather than asking them.

Some people say that curiosity can't be learned. I believe that it can be awakened in anyone and even in well-established, all-too-comfortable organizations. I also believe that active, compulsive curiosity may be the most essential dimension of the future-ready mindstate because creativity and innovation just don't happen without it. Your curiosity will turn you into an intrepid dot collector, an enthusiastic norm challenger, and an insatiable learner—all qualities that produce the new ideas that will give shape to your future. Newton Cheng, Google's Director of Health + Performance, focuses his curiosity on himself to a kind of remarkable effect.

Riding the Wave of Curiosity

NEWTON CHENG

I was raised in a traditional Chinese-Filipino-American family where there was a particular view of what the future should look like for me. My elders—whom I was raised to respect—saw me on a straight path to become a doctor or lawyer or some other kind of professional. I was well into my career as an electrical engineer before I realized how limiting that vision was for me.

I remember walking out of a brutal design review meeting and was told, "Yeah, you're gonna be working through the holidays." Before I could resign myself to several days of work I increasingly disliked, this honest thought popped in my head: *What would I do if I didn't care what my parents think?* Two answers came to me immediately: I'd go buy a bottle of vodka and get loaded. And I'd throw out this career and go do something else. I did both.

I made a blank page of myself and filled it with things I was curious about. For example, throughout my twenties I was a breakdancer, which is a blast but really rough on the body. In my thirties, I was trying to keep it up, but my body was like, "Nope, no more." I was looking for something else to do and went to a gym one day and tried something called a deadlift, where you bend down and pick up a loaded barbell from the floor. I lifted three hundred pounds and was like, "Well, that's pretty good." Then I thought, *Wait, what's the world deadlifting record for some-one of my weight?* A YouTube search led me to a video of Richard Hawthorne, a 132-pound guy who lifted 600 pounds five times to set many world records in his weight class. How could this guy have the same slight build as I did but was able to lift more than four times his own body weight?

With an intense curiosity about what my body was capable of, I set off to master the techniques and discover all the tricks of the world-class deadlifters. Ten years later, I'm lifting 550 pounds, I have won one world championship and four U.S. national championships, and Richard Hawthorne is my friend. This wasn't a swift achievement; the road has been long, but it has refined me physically, mentally, spiritually, and philosophically—all tremendous benefits I could only imagine were out there beyond the horizon.

Curiosity also carried me from the world of engineering to Google and a job I love developing, launching, and scaling global initiatives to help Googlers thrive physically and mentally. When I found myself feeling dangerously burned out in this role, I took a mental health leave to try to understand what had gotten me there. I intended to address my healing through a rigorous schedule of meditation, exercise, reading, and journaling, but this quickly just became another job for me. Ultimately, I had to spend serious time with nothing but white space in my schedule to see where each day would take me. After about three weeks, my brain finally started to quiet down.

I also connected with a few friends I had known in high school and in my early twenties, people who were an especially clear "mirror" that helped me recall parts of me that are core to who I am but that I had put away as I built up this fortress of accomplishments that comprised my career. As I peeled away the façade, I had to reexamine childhood traumas and consider how they might be manifesting as the anxiety that was grappling with my achievement orientation.

This all sounds hard and probably also unpleasant, but I approached it with a kind of tender curiosity that made the effort so valuable and rewarding. I had to be willing—even eager—to understand these facets of myself that were unfamiliar to me. I didn't know what I would discover, I just wanted to be in a frame of mind to explore my own mind.

I know that a lot of people are struggling with similar issues, so I committed to being open about my story when I came back from leave. Right away, requests started coming in from all over for me to speak about mental health and what leaders need to do to address the complex, pervasive problem of burnout. It feels like a kind of movement is taking shape around this, and I will be compelled to be a part of it.

It was scary to let go of my engineering career, but in order to have the new experiences I knew would take me toward the life I wanted to live, I had to let go of stuff that I was holding too tightly. To be curious is to take leaps and plunges that can be a shock to the system, but they also reveal all the opportunities and possibilities that shape a path of purpose.

To ignite curiosity, you learn to acknowledge your personal assumptions, use your senses, and get comfy with what you don't know.

Step Over Your Assumptions

When I first started working at Google, I began a 20 percent side project that I hoped would radically change the employee experience. First, I needed to understand what an employee's typical day was like—where they go, who they talk to, how they engage with their environment. I thought if I could get a vivid picture of how they spent their day, I might be able to identify some ways to improve the way their time was structured, making more space for focus and reflection. For example, I had an idea to put a camera around the necks of a small cohort of people and let the camera show me what their days looked like.

I wanted to use a special camera that was being tested at the time for Alzheimer's patients to take time-lapse photos that might trigger short-term memories. It was a cool piece of equipment, but HR gave me a hard no on my idea to ask other people to wear the camera. In fact, they asked me not to even mention the idea to anyone, which only made me more curious to know what I might learn from it. So I put the camera around my own neck for two weeks, wearing it from the time I got up in the morning until the end of the day, through meetings and meals, traveling back and forth to work, and putting the kids to bed.

Prior to this experiment, I thought I had a pretty clear picture of what I did every day. I mean, how much could there be to account for? You get ready in the morning, drive to the office, meet with some people, have lunch, meet with some more people, sit in front of a screen, go home, eat dinner, play a bit, then go to bed. The photos I reviewed each night told a different story. I did all of those things, of course, but I also did a million other things. And I was exposed to so many details and so much information that never even registered in the moment. When I saw my experience, without the filter of those assumptions, it was more colorful and diverse than I had recognized.

We all operate based on our personal assumptions. These are the stories we tell ourselves to make sense of what happens every day. Our assumptions allow us to move through our daily lives with less friction, but they also create barriers to new insights and experiences. I had no idea how much I was missing by framing my day in such one-dimensional terms. This odd glimpse at my own life showed me some of the really interesting stuff I could have been exploring that I was leaving on the table every day.

Your personal assumptions are different from the practical assumptions we'll consider later in the context of experimentation. Personal assumptions aren't bad, they're just not helpful to you when they're obscuring the threads of curiosity that you might otherwise be following. I think of my personal assumptions as tree roots sticking out of the ground, something that I need to purposely step over to get to everything ahead of me.

Stepping over your personal assumptions boils down to resisting the impulse to make sense of or categorize what you experience. Everything doesn't need to go into a bucket. So many things you encounter every day are actually unique and worthy of your focused interest. When you cast aside all the frames and labels you usually put on the components of your daily life, you immediately begin to see something else, something *new*. Now your curiosity can light on these things and give them a good look.

For years, Shakespeare's *Macbeth* has been staged in unconventional ways that make us confront our own assumptions. It's been set in gangland Chicago, in feudal Japan, in a Seattle high school, in a psychiatric ward, in rural Pennsylvania, and, of course, in the future. Every time the familiar story is tipped this way or that, it causes the audience to set aside its assumptions and look at the play with new eyes.

I once took my son to a Zen monastery in the mountains for a weekend to learn calligraphy, an outing he had chosen for his ninth birthday. Here were our assumptions: We expected we would take classes with an elderly Japanese monk. We assumed that calligraphy would be a fun skill to acquire, like learning to play a musical instrument. We asked ourselves, *How hard could it be to write fancy letters?* And we thought we'd come home with this nifty new trick we could show off to the rest of the family.

What really happened: A middle-aged American calligraphy master greeted us on our arrival. It was fun at first, but it required us to follow a discipline that frustrated us as we learned to look for imperfections over and over again in our strokes. Because this kind of calligraphy is actually a form of art and meditation, we spent the whole weekend working on just a few characters, practicing them over and over while learning to breathe in the moment and accept that each attempt could be better or worse than the last. At home, we hung two modest masterpieces on the wall, each depicting just seven characters, realizing that what we had actually learned over the weekend was patience.

We could have been disappointed by our assumptions not aligning with what we were experiencing. But as we bumped up against each assumption, we decided it was better not to let them keep us from fully exploring what was actually in front of us. Acknowledging and then stepping over these assumptions allowed us to spend time together that surprised and enlightened us both.

Think of a situation you've been in that was clearly framed by your assumptions. A meeting with your boss, a trip to the dentist, a family gathering. To understand how your assumptions influence your experience, start by making a list of the assumptions you have that are associated with the situation. They could be expectations, prejudices, random preconceived notions, or just information you believe to be true. Be honest with yourself and try to name as many assumptions as possible.

Now for each assumption, ask yourself: *Was the assumption based on fact or opinion? Is it possible that the assumption was incorrect? What new information might I have overlooked because of the assumption? How might my experience have been different without the assumption?* When you engage in this exercise after the fact, you can see how your assumptions get in your way. When you make yourself conscious of your assumptions in real time and purposely step over them, you open yourself to where your curiosity may take you.

Unchecked, your assumptions can entirely overwhelm the curious impulse. When the Christian Democratic Union party lost the federal election in Germany in 2021, party leaders contacted me to help them think about how to "reinvent" the party. Under Chancellor Angela Merkel's leadership, the party had dominated German politics for the better part of two decades. Now they were kind of shell-shocked and looking for some big insights that would help them succeed again in subsequent elections.

Although I did not share a political affiliation with this party, I agreed to meet with them because I was interested to hear about their challenges. After a good amount of discussion, I had exactly one insight to share with them: your curiosity is gone. Their polls showed them the same old information in relation to the same old issues that they'd been considering for years. Their assumptions were wrapped tightly around this data and had calcified to such an extent that they had stopped looking for the new and surprising information that might have enabled them to adapt and succeed even in a turbulent political environment.

I conducted a workshop with twenty party leaders to help them reorient their thinking around what they *don't* know and begin asking themselves new questions. At one point, I told them to look around the room and identify a simple item that might represent a metaphor of the future for them. One person chose a blank piece of paper representing the notion that the future is still to be written. Others presented similar objects that suggested letting go or turning a page. You could almost hear some of the hardened assumptions they'd accumulated over the years breaking into little pieces inside their heads. They left our meeting eager to consider their situation in all-new terms.

When I say "step over your assumptions" to get closer to your curiosity, it really is as simple as that: see them for what they are and consciously go beyond them to make your way to the discovery that is just ahead of you.

Investigate Using All Your Senses

Curiosity is triggered by a mystery that may present itself through any of the five senses. Given that we take in about 80 percent of the information we process every day through our eyes, one might fairly expect that our curiosity is piqued primarily through our sense of sight as well. But the compulsively curious are observant on a multi-sensory level, using all of their perceptive abilities to identify opportunities for discovery. They also use all of their senses to investigate the objects of their curiosity, which amplifies their learning.

Each of the senses supplies the brain with critical information, prompts probing questions, and helps us gain useful answers and adapt accordingly to what we've learned. So why do we rely so much on just one of them when we could get so much more from all of them? Sure, we're visual creatures, and our sight provides us with the most immediately actionable information. But each sense delivers unique data that, when combined, give us the richest, most meaningful impression of what we experience.

A half an hour in a garden illustrates this perfectly. You work the soil with your hands to plant new lettuce. You hear bees going about their business among the sunflowers. Your arms are pricked by tiny thorns when you gather raspberries. You smell the fragrant lavender as your leg brushes against it. You spot a lizard taking a bit of shade in a leafy squash patch. You take a bite of a sweet tomato you just picked that's still warm from the sunshine.

There's a whole world of sensory stimuli in that short while in a garden, most of which beg for further investigation. My wife, Angela, is drawn to the simultaneous simplicity and complexity of what happens in the garden, as well as to the continuous observation, experimentation, and adaptation that gardening requires of her. She returns to the garden day after day out of curiosity about what has happened since she was there last and what new things she will learn from the distinct conditions that each day brings. She describes herself as a "grower," an apt term for someone who uses all her senses to understand and nurture a thriving garden and who also grows herself as a result.

You might think that gardening is unique in its involvement of all the senses, but it's not. Think about the last time you went to the movies. The big screen, the surround-sound system, and the popcorn: how it smells when they're making it in the lobby, how it feels when you grab a warm fistful from the bucket, how those first few bites taste. It's also happening at the grocery store, at work, at school, at the airport, in an elevator. You tune out a lot of the sensory information you receive because you don't need all of it in most of these situations. But when you crank up your senses, you become more aware and your curiosity follows.

How exactly can you dial up your sensory engagement? Start by exercising one sense at a time. Using a single sense to process an experience brings a whole different kind of information to your brain.

Eating in total darkness, for example, is a strange but illuminating way to let your sense of taste act as your lead investigator. Since the late 1990s, restaurants all over the world have offered a "dark dining" experience, where you eat your entire meal while wearing a blindfold or in a totally darkened environment. Diners have described the taste of even ordinary food as being more intense and found themselves wondering more about the ingredients in the food they were eating. Their sense of smell was also heightened, as their brains sought more nonvisual information about what they were eating.

Experiment with this approach on your own. Prepare a favorite dish so you can explore it with new (blindfolded) "eyes." Note any fresh impressions you have or questions that pop in your head as you eat. Think of five words that describe what you are tasting. Consider how your blindfolded meal was different from that same meal eaten with your eyes open. Did you eat more slowly or quickly? Did you notice the temperature of the food more or less? Did the meal make you want to prepare the dish differently next time? A shortcut version of this exercise is to eat an ice cream cone or a ripe piece of fruit with your eyes closed.

You can do this with any one of your senses. Watch a movie with the sound off. Close your eyes and take a big, slow whiff of your tea or coffee before you have a sip. Pet your dog with the back of your hand. Take a walk focused just on the ambient sounds. In each case, you will notice at least one thing you otherwise would not have noticed that rolls around in your head for a while and pokes at you until you give in and go off to find out more about it.

Note that you're not seeking the sublime, nor shock and awe. You're just looking for the slightest bit of added depth and detail your multiple senses can contribute to what you discover. You will absolutely encounter some amazing things when you're paying attention with just one of your senses—seeing a hummingbird hovering outside your window can take your breath away. But all the sensory details matter, even the most mundane. Also, there's no good or bad result. You learn as much from a foul smell as from a lovely one.

When you observe, you take in information and make connections and associations based on that information. As such, you can closely observe a situation through any of your senses, say, through your sense of touch as easily as through your sight.

I have trained tens of thousands of people—Googlers and others—on how to observe more comprehensively using more than just what they see. One group of Googlers I worked with was focused on rethinking the hiring and onboarding process, which had become a sore spot at Google over the years. The problems were primarily related to scale (Google onboards hundreds of new employees every week), getting new employees up to speed as quickly as possible (Google is a complex organization), and helping them establish effective networks within the company (a cultural priority for the company).

I encouraged them to look for ways to get as close as possible to the people experiencing challenges within the process (e.g., hiring managers, applicants, interviewers, and onboarding staff). As they sat in on interviews and onboarding sessions, I asked them to collect information about what these new employees (affectionately known as Nooglers) were seeing, saying, hearing, and feeling when partic-ipating in different parts of the process, including several post-onboarding check-in points over the course of a year. Specifically, I asked them to observe every person based on what they were saying or doing, and every situation based on the environment (what could be seen or heard) during different activities. These observations were expected to be authentic (based on empirical evidence), nonobvious (based on fresh multisensory information), and revealing (offering a glimpse of what the Noogler was thinking or feeling).

Later I asked them to look carefully at each of their observations and consider all of the reasons they might be happening. By turning their focus from their observations (what happened) to possible causes, (why it happened) they would begin to see a hundred differ-ent ways to solve these problems with creative solutions.

One interesting observation they brought back was that most Nooglers connected with only eight to ten other people during the earliest onboarding activities, even though they were among hun-dreds of new employees being onboarded together. The Googlers could see these relationships forming based on conversations they heard and on the Nooglers' increasing physical ease with each other and similar clues. Why was this happening? Like the crew you ate lunch with in the first week of high school and then every day for the next four years, simple but powerful and lasting bonds were being formed out of an uncomfortable shared experience.

Knowing that these relationships were the ones most Nooglers maintained beyond the onboarding experience, we could now imagine ways to support the forming of those relationships at the start and sustaining them throughout their tenure with the com-pany. Among a number of initiatives, we started by reconfiguring the onboarding meeting spaces to feature tables that sat ten people instead of individual auditorium-style seating. We began actively encouraging networking as a valuable component of their Google experience. And we pointed them to community-driven groups they could join, such as the Hispanic/LatinX network (HOLA), PRIDE at Google, or the Black Googler Network. There was so much discovered, so many ideas produced, and so much improvement that resulted from looking at this one subject in a multisensory way—almost as if the whole exercise was in color instead of black and white.

Your senses engage your emotions, instincts, and memories, which is what makes them such a potent component of your curiosity. Use them to keep your curiosity crackling.

Change Your Mindstate: Cold

Since ancient Greek and Roman times, cold water immersion has been used for a variety of physical, psychological, and even social reasons. For our purposes, it's a sensory experiment you would try entirely out of curiosity. No need to take a Nordic ice bath or a polar plunge. At the end of your morning shower, turn the water to the coldest possible temperature for sixty seconds. Pay close attention to how it makes your body feel, of course, but also to your own thoughts while it's happening and later as your day progresses. If this experience is interesting to you and you're curious to learn more from it, try it for a week, slightly increasing the amount of time under the cold water each day.

Each time, your brain will tell you not to do this. Each time, you won't know exactly how it will feel or what your immediate or lingering reaction will be. Every experience is unique. The water is the same, but your response will be different. An act of almost pure curiosity, it's a simple exercise that takes you outside your limits.

Get Comfortable
with the Unknown

One of the reasons we let curiosity go dormant as adults is because we discover at a young age that curiosity can get us into trouble. When a child is confronted with a DO NOT TOUCH sign, for example, curiosity inevitably prevails and the results range from illicit pleasure to embarrassment to guilt to one-hundred-proof pain. Go through enough of that and by the time you're a grown-up, you've learned not to touch.

Sadly, the hot-stove wisdom gained from those experiences impacts many of the other ways we might express curiosity. Curiosity becomes comingled with fear in our minds, and we start to avoid situations where we are not sure what will happen. This certainly removes some danger and uncertainty from our lives, but it also keeps us from exploring and learning and discovering what's possible for the future.

How can you break down this resistance you've built against your own curious instinct?

It helps to think for a moment about the concept of the horizon. There's the spatial horizon, that faraway line where the earth and sky seem to meet. This idea is kind of magical and exciting, a tasty cocktail of nature and space and science. Then there's the metaphorical horizon, that much-closer line that marks where your knowledge, interest, and experience end. This idea is not so tasty. It's the reason a well-meaning adult signed you up for sleepaway camp or ballet lessons or immersive French class when you were a kid—to "broaden your horizons."

The spatial horizon represents the beautiful mystery of the unknown. It beckons! The metaphorical horizon seems to point to where your curiosity ran out of steam. I propose we mash up these ideas so you can see your (metaphorical) horizon—your knowledge, interests, and experience—not as the end but as the brilliant and limitless beginning. *This* horizon will draw you out into the unknown, which is exactly where you want to be.

Why is it so hard to say "I don't know"? We don't want to say it to someone else because it makes us feel ignorant or incompetent. We don't like saying it to ourselves because it makes us feel vulnerable or insecure. It's kind of a shame that we spend so much time and energy avoiding saying "I don't know" when the very best spot to find yourself is often with a question mark over your head.

People who are afraid to admit they don't know something also tend to be really good at dodging situations where they won't have all the answers. They rarely venture outside their areas of basic proficiency. This makes their world pretty small. People who are comfortable saying "I don't know" are happy to be the newbie. They have no boundaries, no lanes, no boxes to confine them. They live in a much bigger world.

Imagine yourself as a native in the land of the unknown. You roam about the terrain unsure of what you will encounter but confident you'll figure it out. You eschew maps and directions—relying on your instincts instead is exhilarating and makes you more attentive to what you see along the way. You use what you know and what you don't know to explore and enrich your experience. You're alert and observant, growing in your knowledge and capability every day.

How do you get to the land of the unknown? Start by actively putting yourself in situations where you have no previous knowledge or experience that would help you understand or acclimate to what's happening. Be the proverbial blank slate. If you're not aware of the history behind it or its guiding principles or other contextual information, you will be perfectly surprised and take in information solely through your perceptions.

Googler Sarah Brown likens this to trying on someone else's glasses. "Everybody walks around wearing a pair of glasses that causes them to see the world in a particular way," she explains.

"I like to ask powerful questions that get someone to put on different glasses and experience a new perspective. They think, *Oh, the world doesn't have to be this one way; it could actually be this other way.*"

Go as far away from your own experience as you can. An easy way to do this is to go someplace you've never once thought of visiting, maybe another part of the country or different part of the world. Closer to home, you might attend a religious or cultural event that is entirely outside of your own experience. Or volunteer with an organization that represents a cause that has never touched you before.

A friend once offered his time to a nonprofit helping Somali immigrants get settled in his Midwestern state. He knew nothing of their history—he didn't even know where to find Somalia on a map. First through interpreters and later in their burgeoning English, he listened to stories of their homeland, their journey to this country, and the challenges they faced assimilating here. Over the months he worked with them, his empathy and resilience were amplified by his immersion in a world that was previously unfamiliar to him.

I can't overstate the value of letting your curiosity take you to parts unknown. Every time you go there, you get more comfortable being there. In fact, it makes you want to go there again and again. And what you learn there will always grow some important part of you in an unexpected way.

Change Your Mindstate: Mars

Often when I'm working with a group that's trying to power through to a solution to a problem, I encourage them to stop and take an "inspiration walk." This is just a short, mindful stroll outdoors that's meant to shift the brain from idea output mode to creative input mode.

To shift from "what I know" to "what I don't know" mode, take a walk on Mars. You don't even need to get out of your chair to do this. Use Google Earth's Voyager feature to simulate a walk on the red planet or a climb up El Capitan or a swim alongside a whale shark.[3] Or go to a YouTube virtual reality channel and surf a monster wave. Putting yourself someplace else—in this case, someplace *very* else—tips your perspective and may even disorient you in a positive way.

Be amazed as often as possible. Being in a state of wonder makes the ordinary special and attracts all kinds of intriguing things into your line of sight. When you're in a state of wonder, you're more likely to be surprised by the world around you. The element of surprise more than triples the intensity of any emotion, which is why your heart pounds with fear when someone pops out of a closet during a scary movie. It's also why you get a rush of pleasure when you are surprised by something positive. Anything from the sudden appearance of a rainbow after a thunderstorm to a text out of the blue from someone you've been thinking about can give you that happy jolt. You can't anticipate a surprise, of course—that's what makes it a surprise. But pay attention to how a surprise makes you feel and how long that feeling stays with you.

When someone performs a magic trick, is your first instinct to try to figure out how the heck they did that? Or do you let yourself savor the magic part? Sometimes you need to resist the urge to be rational in order to expose yourself to interesting stuff you can't explain. Take space, example. Humans have been looking up at the night sky with awe and wonder since the beginning of time. We've also spent many centuries trying to figure out what's out there, how it all works. We've learned plenty of things, but there's much more we don't know. On the one hand, it's thrilling every time curiosity leads us to learn something new about space. On the other, it's just as thrilling to think that we could never figure it all out. Knowing we are a part of this supremely unknowable universe is exactly the point.

Entrepreneur and former Googler Jon Ratcliffe's curiosity compels him to keep asking questions without fear of where the answers will take him.

Getting Good at Not Having the Answers
JON RATCLIFFE

When I left Google in 2015 to start my own video production company, my motivations were very different from what makes me want to be an entrepreneur today. The things I thought would bring me joy then are completely different from the things that actually do bring me joy now. When I started out, I wanted to show the world what I was capable of, do great things, make a bunch of money. I didn't know how much pain I would go through before finding out what really mattered to me.

There were about ten people on my team when I realized none of them was inspired by what we were doing together. I was leading them, but I wasn't helping them feel excited about our work. A friend said to me at the time, "You have to stop being the greatest player of all time and instead be the greatest coach of all time." He was right. We were three years in, and I was still trying to make all the plays and score all the goals for the business. I was being the hero leader instead of the empowering and inspiring leader. It was awful to realize that I'd brought these smart, capable people along on my entrepreneurial journey and they were unhappy because of me.

An existential crisis ensued. I was literally asking myself, *Why should our company even exist? If we're not creating the best product AND the best work environment and culture, what is this company here for?* I came to realize that how I played my role as a leader had a direct impact on my team's happiness and sense of purpose, and that their state of mind was connected to my state of mind. If I could get my head right, theirs would follow.

I worked hard on the why of our company. I had to ask a lot of questions that I wasn't sure I'd like the answers to. I had to make peace with the possibility that what I discovered might point to a very different outcome than what I had in my head when I left Google. But I had to know, no matter what I learned.

We're fifty people now, and it surprises me every day how much joy I get from leading this group. What makes our culture so special is that it doesn't come from me—it comes from other people in the organization who understand where we want to go and then take us there. Even the most junior person on the team brings their great questions and ideas to every conversation, and as a result, our product has rapidly evolved and improved.

Our company is in a very competitive space. We can't survive by staying still. Our product always has to look different than it did the year before, which is why our curiosity about what's possible out there has become so core to the company's success. You can have eight years of great business, then in year nine, you lose your curiosity and your product will just flatline.

I believe that to be curious, you have to be ready and willing to dive into the big waves. I had been intrigued by Archbishop Desmond Tutu for a long time, and one day in 2011 I wrote to his office saying, "Hey, I work for Google, and if there's ever anything I can help you with I hope you'll call me." The very next day, they contacted me and said, "Well, maybe you can help us. His Holiness the Dalai Lama was supposed to travel to South Africa in three days to participate in an event for Archbishop Tutu's birthday, but his visa has been held up for political reasons. Is it possible we could use technology to do this another way?"

Google Hangouts was still in development at the time, but I called Gopi Kallayil, the head of brand marketing for Google+ at the time and a spiritual seeker himself, to ask if he could help me.

Even though we had never met and I'd woken him out of a sound sleep, he said, "You know, the impossible takes one or two days. Miracles take slightly longer, maybe three days. Let's do this." Sixty hours later, a handful of Googlers from India, South Africa, Sweden, and the United States teamed up to make it happen.

The event was to take place at the University of the Western Cape, where we had set up Archbishop Tutu's equipment (a couple of laptops and some cable we hoped would provide a stable Internet connection). Six thousand miles away in India, another Googler had driven twelve hours from New Delhi to the Dalai Lama's home in the Himalayas to rig the same setup. Despite a power outage in Cape Town fifteen minutes before the event and the high risk of technical failure on both ends, the two men met via Google Hangouts for an hour-long conversation about compassion and their enduring friendship.

Thousands of people around the world watched this momentous meeting in real time on their own computers, which today seems unremarkable but in 2011 was pretty wow. And it really was a miracle, born not of technology but of curiosity—mine, Archbishop Tutu's and the Dalai Lama's, Gopi's, and that of the dozen Googlers who pulled off this crazy caper. It's what's possible when you're intent on learning something regardless of what might happen when you do.

Find a Question

We have grown accustomed to posing questions expecting to find immediate answers (thanks, Google!). But for the compulsively curious, getting the answer or solving the problem quickly isn't the point (sorry, Google!). In fact, the content of the question isn't even the point. The act of questioning is the point.

Neurologist and philosopher Erwin Strauss described human beings as "question animals," creatures who are unique in their natural instinct and ability to ask questions.[4] He also said that a person's questions are as revealing as their dreams because they come from the same rich historical, cultural, and social reservoir. When we ask a question, we are just articulating a conscious (and subconscious) desire to know more—we're expressing our curiosity.

Two simple words that you say to yourself are the essence of curiosity: I wonder. I wonder why . . . I wonder what would happen if . . . I wonder how . . . I wonder what's inside this box . . . I wonder what's underneath this rock . . . I wonder where my future will take me . . .

Those ellipses that follow every "I wonder" are like Skittles that will lead you to your answers, but only if you don't let the thought flit away from you as "I wonders" often do. Hold on to it for a little while. As it tumbles around in your head, it will take you to some odd and wonderful places. Eventually you'll find yourself starting down a trail that will lead to a number of answers and even more questions. Every step you take on that trail is a choice. Many steps = many choices = many pieces of information you didn't have before. All this creative input expands your sense of what's possible. From here, you can begin to imagine and see the shape of the future you want to build.

I fell hard for California in 2000 when I came to Cal State Long Beach as an undergraduate for a semester abroad. For nearly eight months, I slept on an air mattress on the floor of a friend's apartment, but all I could think was, *How can I stay here a little longer?* Eventually I had to go home to Germany, but in 2009 I was happy to make my way back to California when I took a research position at Stanford. At this point, I didn't know what my career was going to look like, but the idea of making my home here was starting to take hold in my head.

One day, Angela and I decided to visit Googleplex, Google's

corporate headquarters that everyone talked so much about. We went into the visitors' welcome building and asked the receptionist if there was a tour of the campus that we could join. She laughed and pointed to three buttons on the sign-in monitor on the counter. They read: INTERVIEW, BUSINESS APPOINTMENT, and SOCIAL APPOINTMENT. She said the only way you can see the campus is if you're here for one of these reasons.

I remember thinking, *I want to press the* INTERVIEW *button.* Eleven months later, I was standing in the same spot talking to a different receptionist and tapping the INTERVIEW button on the screen. In those eleven months, the picture of what I wanted my future to look like became clearer every day. It wasn't a picture of me working for Google, it was a picture made up of all the threads of my curiosity coming together.

One of the classes I have taught at the Stanford d.school consists of six weeks solely devoted to finding a question. At the end of the class, we set up a "questroom" where students would display an artifact of their question and a description of their question-finding experience. One student's question—"How can we produce clothing more sustainably?"—was presented alongside five T-shirts. Next to each shirt was a sign explaining where it was produced, how many people participated in its production, and what materials and chemicals were used to make the shirt. Together, these simple snapshots showed quite dramatically that the way these shirts are made isn't sustainable at all.

One of my students, a supersmart PhD candidate, told me this was the most difficult class he had taken because he was not allowed even to think about possible answers to the questions he was considering.

Allow your curiosity to stretch your questions so they reach ahead of you into the future. If your question is focused on something right in front of you, consider how you might expand it to encompass something bigger or something that hasn't happened yet. When I first came to California, I asked, *I wonder how can I stay here a little longer?* That question stretched when I later asked, *I wonder how can I press that* INTERVIEW *button?* Then, *I wonder what impact can I have on one of the most innovative companies in the world?* and eventually, *I wonder how can I raise a family here?*

Change Your Mindstate: Upside Down

Sometimes getting to the best answer requires you to be curious enough to ask a rogue question. First look at the problem you're trying to solve. Say you're getting anxious because sales of your top product have been flat for months. You've been pestering your team with the question "How can we increase sales?" They keep answering with the usual responses—marketing, advertising, consumer research, etc. Now ask instead, "What can we do to decrease sales?"

The discussion that follows this upside-down question will be lively and illuminating. It will point to issues you hadn't considered and ultimately to the answers you're looking for along with some others you weren't looking for at all.

Try this on any area of your life. If you're in a personal relationship that's hit a rough patch, ask yourself, *What could I do to make this relationship worse?* You will quickly identify behaviors or patterns of communication that may be the source of the problem in the relationship. Or maybe you're feeling a high level of stress or anxiety. Ask yourself, *What could make me feel more overwhelmed?* Or you're struggling with a difficult decision, such as whether to accept a new job you've been offered. Instead of asking yourself, *Should I take this job?* ask yourself, *What will happen if I don't take this job?* Upside-down questions help to surface truths and realities that the questions you think you should be asking often don't.

When your curiosity is engaged, it's as powerful a motivator as any of your most primal needs or desires. It will drive you to seek and find for the sake of your own personal satisfaction and growth. And with apologies to the well-worn phrase "satisfy one's curiosity," compulsive curiosity can never be satisfied. It becomes a never-ending quest to learn and experience more that expands you from the inside out.

Fair warning: it takes courage to be curious. Society has always frowned on curiosity because it often causes people to break the rules or ask uncomfortable questions. Yes, curiosity is a threat to the established order. And it may well put you at odds with institutions of authority or even with your own values. But progress and innovation can't happen without it.

The curious path isn't straight. It meanders and doglegs and changes course right beneath your feet. It can lead you to dead ends and contradictions that you may mistake for failure to find an answer. But this is what makes your curiosity one big, bold, dot-collecting expedition. You gather all this creative input—a blizzard of dots—that your imagination shapes into the path toward your future.

Do
you
        DIS-
COVER
        opportu-
nity

every

        day?

Try This

Turn this book into something else.

Use it as a tool.

Or make music with it.

Or wear it.

Is this book more than a book?

CHAPTER 5

Perpetual Experimen- tation

Perpetual experimentation fuels immediate discovery. It tests ideas rapidly and repeatedly and keeps pressing you toward where the learning leads. You're not looking for an epic epiphany, you're looking for lots of little insights that lead to new ideas.

The day I met my wife, Angela, for the first time, I told her, "This will be an extraordinary relationship." She laughed and asked how I could be so sure. "I don't know it for a fact, but I have this feeling," I answered.

Later, I wondered how I might determine quickly and definitively whether the relationship really could be extraordinary. You usually figure that out over an extended period of time getting to know each other—you know, dating! But I didn't want to go through months or years of trial and error. I had an idea to test this new relationship early to find out if we each might be the partner the other was looking for.

Angela first looked at me sideways when I explained my idea. But she really liked the notion of "testing" the relationship to understand the potential between us. So just a month after meeting, we decided to explore our relationship by taking a three-week road trip in a country neither of us had ever visited. We embarked with no itinerary or plans, just our backpacks and a good amount of hope for this new friendship.

We quickly learned what it was like to be together 24/7 in unfamiliar situations. We learned we both have a passion for exploring nature, local markets, and food. On a tough nighttime mountain climb, we learned we could mentally and physically rely on each other. We learned that even when we were hungry and tired, we could still laugh about the situations in which we found ourselves. Most important to both of us, by the end of our trip, we knew that we would be able to solve any challenge we encountered by facing it together.

Admittedly, this experience was unusual by traditional relationship development standards, but this intense three-week outing allowed us to conduct an invaluable experiment. We basically prototyped our relationship to determine whether it was something that would work and was what we wanted. It turns out that it did work and it was what we wanted—we married in 2010 and have built an extraordinary relationship based on the results of that experiment.

Of all of the dimensions of the future-ready mindstate, **perpetual experimentation** is the most purposeful and action oriented. You're not just thinking about something, you're getting out there and doing it. Which ought to make it the easiest dimension to strengthen, right? It should be like going to the gym—you commit to doing it, you do it regularly, and over time, you develop bigger muscles.

In some ways, this is true. It is most like a positive habit or behavior you can choose to establish, and it can clearly deliver the benefit of doing so. But for some, experimentation may actually be the toughest dimension to cultivate, considering you may have spent a lifetime actively or subconsciously avoiding doing it.

The instinct to explore and experiment comes naturally to us as children. At first, we're impervious to obstacles in our quest to explore. But over time, this experimental nature becomes stifled by fear—fear of danger or pain, fear of the unknown, or fear of failure. Unfortunately, parents and other influential adults in a child's life are largely responsible for tamping down this dimension almost from the start. Believe me, I know that a parent's most important job is to help kids survive their own childhoods. But in the process of protecting them, we inadvertently teach them to avoid experiences that aren't certain or safe. As a result, they grow up to be adults who have forgotten how to experiment.

I'm here to tell you that the road to the future is paved with experiments. Countless, endless experiments. Small, silent, invisible experiments and big, bold, loud experiments. Too many people carry around the notion that experimentation is for scientists or creatives, when in fact, it's an enormously powerful tool we all have at our disposal—no lab coat required. Ultimately, experimentation is how every one of us can break from where we are now to discover what's possible ahead.[1]

Experimentation is first and foremost a way of thinking. It's an inclination toward action versus stasis and the unknown versus the known. It requires that openness to experience that is a fundamental dimension of the future-ready mindstate, along with a healthy dose of curiosity that instills excitement and imagination.

Say you find yourself in a room that is entirely unfamiliar to you.

In this room, there is a closed door. Would you look around for someone to give you permission to open the door? Would you wait for someone to come through the door? Or would you just open the door to find out what's behind it?

No question, the action-oriented explorers would reach for the doorknob right away. And if they found it was locked, they'd want to figure out how to get inside anyway. Everyone else would be constrained by a lack of curiosity (who cares what's behind the door?) or a fear of consequences (what if something bad is behind the door?). The experimental way of thinking sees opportunity and potential behind every closed door.

Why is experimentation so hard?

One reason is that our brains tend to want to save energy, so we go with ideas and solutions that have worked in the past or shy away from new approaches that may be challenging. We cling to the familiar even when we're aware that the familiar might not actually be that great. We make choices every day to stay with what we know rather than to seek new and possibly better experiences. Over a lifetime, we constrain ourselves further and further to exert the least amount of effort and preserve this false sense of safety.

But what if all of your daily decisions were instead intended to *avoid* familiarity and habitual behavior? You'll quickly realize that most of what you experience or encounter is a kind of delightful surprise. You'll also get a little addicted to the kick of discovery, I happen to know for a fact.

Another reason we avoid experimenting is fear of failure. We tend to assume that the objective of experimentation is success, which sets the bar prohibitively high right out of the gate. The fear of failure has such a paralyzing effect on some people that they make no effort at all. If I don't try, I won't fail, right? The fact is, the objective of experimentation is not success, it's simply learning. Each time you try something new, you learn something new. Shifting this one per-ception about experimentation from being focused on success to being focused on learning will make you more open to discovery on every level.

We also struggle with experimentation because we don't want to be disappointed. What if I try a new restaurant and it's not as good as I hoped it would be? Better to stick with my regular restaurant (and the same dish I order every time) than to roll the dice on a new experience. The better question is "What pleasure or insight might I gain from trying the new restaurant?" If you focus on the opportunity, the fear of disappointment loses its power.

For years, Google has conducted an annual employee survey called "Googlegeist" that is intended to take the pulse of the organization and gather Googlers' unvarnished opinions on subjects ranging from the company's mission, leadership, and global citizenship to engagement, compensation, and job satisfaction. Nearly 90 percent of employees participate in Googlegeist, which is an extraordinary response rate for an employee survey.

When the results are released to employees, the three lowest-scoring areas are flagged and Googlers in whatever role or location are encouraged to experiment with their teams on ways to make meaningful, measurable changes in these areas over the course of the following year. One year, the Googlegeist results showed a very low score on the subject of well-being, which to another organization might be a hint that a run for the exits is in the offing. For Google, it resulted in the birth of gPause, a program promoting meditation and mindfulness that has produced a number of signature initiatives that have been adopted in Google offices around the world. You have to be genuinely unafraid of bad news or disappointment to put yourself out there the way Googlegeist does for Google.

So how can you resist your own bias against experimentation and relearn how to experiment as fearlessly and naturally and continuously as you did when you were a child? You get better at living in the realm of possibility, testing and prototyping, taking risks, and letting go.

What If

Experimentation is a deliberate act entirely focused on illuminating what's possible. Every experiment forces you to move toward the unknown, which is the beauty and thrill of it. At the same time, each step brings more clarity that allows you to move forward with purpose. Even when you experiment just for the sake of a fresh perspective, you expand your ability to see the world from a different angle. Each time you do this, you open yourself a little more to the potential for innovation.

When I was a child, I spent many hours in my grandfather's garage, where I made stuff out of all kinds of odds and ends he squirreled away there. Even then, I was aware of how this quirky place made me feel free to create. I've always been a physical space enthusiast, intrigued by the impact a person's immediate environment has on them, especially when it's a shared space.

In my early days at Google, I was surprised to find that for all the play spaces available to employees (remember the ball pits and foosball tables?), there was a lack of workspaces where folks could imagine and experiment. I connected with four other people who had an interest in creative spaces to think about how an experimentation-friendly environment might support Googlers who wanted to pursue their 20 percent projects.

Given the go-ahead to create such a space, we fell into experimentation mode ourselves. What if we didn't design the space at all, but instead watched the Googlers define how the space would be used? We made tables on wheels out of whiteboard surfaces so they could communicate ideas quickly on a horizontal surface and move easily around the room. When they indicated an interest in 3D printing and laser cutting, we incorporated that technological capability into the space. One day we set up a sewing machine in the space just to see what would happen. That was one hot piece of equipment!

We wanted to be scrappy, to try things out quickly. We set up time-lapse cameras so we could see how areas were being used, then adapted based on what was working or not. Inspired by my experience as a child, I suggested we go to a junkyard and get a bunch of old auto parts to set around the space. Eventually this place—which came to be known as "The Garage"—became a favorite spot on the Google campus for brainstorming, talks, concerts, and other creator gatherings.

I hesitate to describe our efforts as "creating" this space because the space kind of created itself. All we wanted to do was to find ways to remove the friction between having an idea and making it real, to allow Googlers to prototype their ideas as a first step toward innovation. By experimenting on an experimentation space—so meta, I know—we discovered a lively balance between chaos and order that inspired the best kind of risky behavior. We learned that people like to touch things and move things around and even break things if they can learn from it. Because the space is fluid and flexible, no one ever settles into the same old spot to do the same old thing.

The Garage has become a model for how an environment can influence innovation, so much so that I've been asked by numerous organizations to replicate a similar innovation space for them. As important as an environment can be to encourage experimentation, creating an innovation space doesn't make innovation happen, any more than putting a paintbrush in someone's hand makes them an artist. It's what's going on in that space between your ears that leads to innovation—your fully engaged mindstate sets the stage.

Change Your Mindstate: Door

Our environment is fundamental to our experimental state of mind, yet it's often only environmental extremes that get our attention.

To focus on the more subtle aspects of your environment, choose a moment when you're about to walk through a door, pause for just a beat, and then take one breath. As you step through the door, try to account for any differences you may be feeling in the space you enter. Does the light or temperature or ambient sound get your attention? What about the density or openness of the space? The door part of this exercise is just meant to remind you to pause and acknowledge that you are about to have a different experience. Play with this idea over time and you won't need the door to stimulate your awareness of what happens when you transition from one space to another. Discovering something new from the physical and mental spaces you enter or leave behind can help to decrease apprehension and other roadblocks to experimentation.

Most people think innovation starts with a great idea, but the truth is that it usually starts with a great question. What if we didn't produce any waste at all? What if we abandoned the "normal" circadian rhythm to eat and sleep and work at any time of the day or night? What if there were no borders in the world?

When was the last time you asked one of these kinds of big, crazy questions out loud? Kids ask audacious questions all the time. Undaunted by practical constraints, they constantly dare to wonder, *What if . . . ?* Natural visionaries never grow out of this way of seeing the world. At the risk of sounding childlike, they ask giant, wide-open questions that challenge the status quo and inspire others to consider what is possible.

In 2016, some folks from NASA came to see me at Google for a "10x thinking" session, an intense brainstorming approach intended to improve something by a factor of ten rather than small increments. After a number of years of waning support in Washington, the agency was in a tough spot. For the first time in its nearly sixty-year history, NASA did not have a mandate for human space exploration. They had all of these world-class astronauts and scientists and billions of dollars of equipment and no missions to train or plan for. To me, they seemed discouraged and their spark to innovate was gone.

Their visit to The Garage was meant to give these NASA leaders, engineers, and designers an opportunity to collaborate with Googlers to reignite their creativity and think about other challenges they might be uniquely skilled to tackle. Like many organizations, NASA had tremendous financial resources and infrastructure to innovate but had drifted away from the big "what if" curiosity that had defined it in its heyday. For their workshop session, they chose an exercise that had nothing to do with space—they wanted to focus on re-imagining cities.

Inspired by the geodesic domes built in the '70s and by the documentary "Spaceship Earth," they explored how to create a self-sustaining environment on Earth to anticipate what it would take to do the same on Mars. They went on to consider other "what ifs," including mitigating loneliness for a human traveling to Mars, promoting space travel for civilians, and reengineering rockets to be used for takeoffs and landings to make space exploration more sustainable. It was fun to see them get excited to reconnect with the power of their own curiosity and think moonshot-big again.

Unfortunately, most of the institutions that shape us—education, government, work, to name just a few—insist that we deliver sure-thing answers and report short-term progress rather than take the time to explore huge questions. Yet to discover new ideas, we have to embrace the uncomfortable process of letting the questions and experimentation lead us. There's no way of knowing where these questions will take things in the long run. But they fuel our optimism and eventually, when the experimentation that flows from these questions leads to innovative breakthroughs, the formerly unimaginable actually happens.

Find the Safety Zone

It's not just fear of failure that keeps us from experimenting. Many people don't ask bold questions and then venture to find the answers because they're afraid of how others will respond. Laughter, awkward silence, derision, rejection, or worse—just ask Galileo. Numerous studies of team dynamics[2] have shown that members of highly functioning teams feel safe to voice their opinions or concerns and to share their ideas. When someone feels this level of psychological safety, they feel more confident to speak their mind and take risks.

Feeling free and supported to experiment requires the same sense of security. The learning that comes from experimentation can be messy—no one wants to feel judged by others for making a mess.[3] Just knowing that you are safe to wonder out loud or try unconventional things out in the open increases your inclination to experiment.

Pixar Animation Studios is an organization whose culture openly fosters psychological safety. Believing that a lack of honest exchange leads to mediocrity and dysfunction, early on the studio founders established the Braintrust meeting, a regular gathering of Pixar filmmakers that is focused on working through problems they're having on their projects. The defining feature of these meetings is total candor, which for a room full of passionate creatives, you can imagine might be a little hard to swallow.

Over the more than thirty years since Pixar was founded, this meeting has become a cornerstone of their development process. Instead of feeling threatened by honest feedback from their peers, the filmmakers use it to overcome the creative blind spots or storytelling obstacles that each of them has experienced many times before. One reason it works so well is because these conversations focus on the project, not the person with the problem. They approach the subject as if they're a bunch of mechanics standing around the open hood of a car trying to figure out why the engine is rattling. No ego, just "What do we need to do to fix this thing?"

In a Braintrust meeting, what would normally be perceived as painful criticism becomes straightforward technical assistance from people whose insights are valued and trusted. This kind of psychological safety is critical to being open to experimentation. It's not only true in a group setting, though—you also need to feel safe in your own head. How many times have you toyed with the idea of doing something different, then talked yourself out of it? We rarely give ourselves permission to move beyond the norm. We tend to seek that permission from others, who more often than not will try to convince us to give up our "crazy ideas."

Usually with the best intentions, the people in our lives will try to protect us from the consequences of our choices. But this doesn't make us safer, it makes us less confident to try new things. How can you create an environment—in your head, in your family, in the various communities of which you're a part—where you feel safe to take risks and experiment?

I've been hacking the answer to this question for many years. When I was a teenager, I had a notion that living in lots of places and trying different jobs would let me discover what my interests and strengths were. My parents were not super happy about this scheme, but I saw this experiment as a personal necessity, a testing of my current self that would shape my future self. My parents saw it as unnecessarily risky, and they weren't wrong about that. I had plenty of trepidation myself, usually when I would realize I was operating without a safety net again, say, starting a new job in a country where I didn't speak the language.

Despite not fully supporting what I was doing, my parents did something that allowed me to find the psychological safety to keep hurtling myself into the unknown: they said, "Whatever you do, we're going to leave your room just as it is so you know that you can always come home if things don't go the way you hoped."

This is exactly what I mean by creating an environment in your head that makes you feel safe to experiment. Finding that very personal inner affirmation—in this case, it was something I could actually visualize—made me feel secure to keep going, regardless of all the (often good) reasons people suggested for returning to a conventional path. It was generous of my parents to offer this comfort, given their constant concern during the years of my travels. It not only helped me accomplish that particular goal, but also provided an excellent model for the kind of psychological safety that I would require from myself to experiment throughout my life.

Fast-forward to 2010, when I was a candidate to join Google to help design learning environments to support leadership and innovation. I had participated in fourteen traditional interviews over nearly four months and as a final challenge was asked to design an original learning experience that would be scalable for ten thousand Googlers. Considering the organization I was looking to become a part of and the nature of the job itself, I felt compelled to respond to this challenge in a unique way. I decided to videotape my process of ideating, prototyping, and delivering a proposed solution.

Over the course of a week, I created a time-lapse video that featured me wearing different-colored T-shirts to represent the different stages of my process, explaining my thinking as I progressed. When I look at it now, I can see the video had a bit of a sleepless, mad-scientist vibe to it—at one point, I even had to borrow a shirt from my wife because I ran out of colored shirts. On the one hand, I knew there was a chance my presentation might miss the mark with the folks on the receiving end. On the other, I felt entirely safe in my own head to openly experiment in this way. I got the job.

It's critical also to prioritize psychological safety for experimentation within the groups you're part of and working with. Be openly supportive of others to experiment, of course, but also actively advocate for it within the families, teams, and organizations with which you're associated. Demonstrating the behavior—supporting experimentation and experimenting yourself—is the best form of advocacy wherever you are.

Every step you take as you experiment strengthens your confidence. When others see you experimenting and learning as you go, they begin to trust the path you're forging, which encourages you forward. (They are also likely to feel encouraged to try some new experiments themselves.) At the beginning of each term at Stanford, we use a creative agency assessment tool to test how comfortable the students are in showing their unfinished work to one another. We invariably discover a high level of apprehension at the start, but as the semester goes on, the students become more comfortable openly sharing rough ideas. They come to realize the value of gathering and offering early feedback and how it helps them make decisions as they go. When we assess them again at the end of the semester, they are infinitely more confident, having built the muscles that allow them to experiment out loud.

Tom Chi was the Head of Experience for Google X during a period of intense product development and knows well how experimentation creates momentum.

Playing the Experimentation Game

TOM CHI

I was born in Taiwan and immigrated to the United States with my family when I was two years old. For the next couple of years, I learned some words in Chinese and English, but nobody was actively teaching me either language, so when I started school, I was basically nonverbal. Without language, I saw the world through numbers and pictures. I made my way to language slowly over the next few years, which I realize now allowed me to enjoy an unusually long period of time without applying the abstractions of language in my life. As a result, from an early age, I saw problems visually and tried to solve them in a hands-on versus a conceptual way. This ended up being very formative for my career, as I saw how words and abstractions can get you lost if they're not a perfect fit for all the nuances of the physical thing you're trying to make. I have built tons of things and taught people to build things and have found that numbers and pictures usually get you closer to what it takes to make that thing.

When I'm kicking off a project, I say, "Okay, here's where you are today. And there's where you're hoping to end up in the future." But you don't know how to get from here to there. And you're worried you're going to pick the wrong path or get lost going from here to there. So let's break it down like a game.

Say I hand you a single die. If you roll a six, you win the game and I will pay you a million dollars. Cool game, right? But if you roll anything other than a six, you lose the game and have to pay me a million dollars. Now you don't want to play because the risk and cost of losing is too high.

Okay, now what if you get to roll the die twenty times? If you roll a six, you win. If you don't roll a six after twenty tries, you lose. So now you're like, "Sure, I'll play that game." I say, "Great, that's an improvement." You went from paralyzed to feeling like you might win. But if by roll seventeen or eighteen, you haven't hit a six, you're sweating.

There's another version of the game where you get to roll a hundred times. With a hundred rolls—whether it's the second roll, the seventeenth roll, or the fifty-first roll—at some point you're going to win the game. Now your confidence is off the charts. Guess what? This is the game you're already playing.

Between where you are right now and what you need to learn to get where you're going, there is some number of iterations you are going to go through to win the game. The only way to lose this game is to take no action. If you take action, there's a 100 percent guarantee you will either crack the problem or learn that what you're doing isn't the way to go and why. Both outcomes are a win because, however many times you roll, you will always end up in a better spot. You just need to be prepared to roll it again and again and again.

On day one of the Google Glass project, I told my team we were going to do fifteen hardware prototypes a week for ten weeks. With three people, this amounted to one prototype per person per day. With such rapid experimentation, my team didn't get attached to the outcome of any experiment because they knew they'd be doing a different one tomorrow. This let them move neutrally and fluidly from one experiment to the next.

The leadership team on the project was not so open. They were stuck on certain ideas—their conjectures—from the start and when we'd present findings that conflicted with their ideas, they'd say, "No, go back and try it again." I thought, *We just showed you that the actual result of the experiment was garbage, but instead of trying something else you want us to keep trying that thing that didn't work? That's not how you learn things.*

On any given day, I'd be flipping between my team saying, "Here are three new experiments we did today," and the leadership team saying, "But what about XYZ idea we had two months ago?" My team was producing actuals at an incredible pace, but the leadership team was just clinging to their conjecture. At one point, they said, "Why aren't we moving forward on XYZ idea?" And I said, "Because we tested extensively on that point for three weeks and the actuals showed that the idea was a no-go." We were providing tons of data they could use to make different decisions, but they were stubbornly stuck in their frame and didn't want to be convinced of anything else.

Everything I learned from that experience can be summed up in my three mantras about experimentation:

1. Conjectures become experiments, and actuals become decisions.
2. Attachment is the enemy of innovation.
3. Specificity is the friend of innovation.

Specificity relates to how to define an experiment's success. Lots of times, people get focused on the popularity of their experiment. If people didn't like my experiment, I lose. If they loved my experiment, I win. Okay, let's say everybody loved it. Without any specifics beyond that fact, I have no idea what to do next with it or how to improve on it.

Say I test a prototype and the user says, "Yeah, that was nice." If you don't press them for specifics about why they like it, you won't learn the more important information about which parts of the experience were satisfying and which were frustrating. That information—the specificity—may not be the flashy stuff that wins the popularity contest, but it instantly drives me to a clear next step. It creates the force of forward motion that is the whole purpose of experimentation.

After I left Google, I launched a consulting business and taught a whole bunch of people what I know about rapid experimentation and prototyping. Then I started a venture capital firm that invests in companies that "help humanity become a net positive to nature." All our investments are about radically shifting the relationship between humanity and nature and disrupting the aspects of the industrial economy that are destroying nature. For example, we're funding a start-up that has developed a honeybee vaccine that will combat the virus that's killing off bee colonies in dangerous numbers. I'm realistic knowing that what I hope to accomplish will take longer than my lifetime. For now, I get to share in the experimental learning with these companies that inhabit this wide frontier of possibility for the future. It's a very fun job.

Test, Prototype, Repeat

Experimentation is all about having a future vision, testing your practical assumptions about that vision, and learning what works and what doesn't. Specifically, experimentation helps you:

- Change opinions into facts
- Prove or disprove your assumptions
- Discover surprises about your audience
- Make more informed decisions
- Use data to tell your story

Testing and prototyping are based on the premise that there is no failure in experimentation, only learning. They help you maximize your rate of learning—quite simply, the more you try, the more you learn. Testing allows you to gather data rapidly that informs your decision to tweak an idea, proceed with it, or let it go. Prototyping reveals two critical pieces of information before you invest too much in an idea: whether it's desirable and whether it works. In short, testing and prototyping comprise the path from not knowing something to knowing it for sure.

How? Using a rapid experimentation loop, you first identify your "leap of faith" (LOF) assumption, the practical assumption that feels most essential to the success of your idea. By practical assumption, I mean something you believe to be true about how something might work. Then you experiment using the absolute minimum resources necessary to test that assumption. When assessing the outcome, note whether your practical assumption held up or not, and any surprises you observed or new insights you discovered. Then decide if you will pivot and change your idea, or preserve your idea and continue to experiment.

To test an idea, you try lots of different approaches, and you try them in quick succession to learn what works and what doesn't. Then you use that learning to inform subsequent tests that refine your idea further or even transform it entirely. But first you have to out your assumptions.

Generally, our worldview is made up of millions of assumptions we have compiled based on past experience. Instead of having a gut reaction to everything that happens to us, we filter each experience through our assumptions and choose our reaction accordingly. In everyday life, we rarely test our own assumptions, partly because it would be massively time-consuming to do so and partly because there's a chance we'll discover something we don't want to know or see.

The sea of assumptions in which we exist gives us comfort and a sense of certainty—no wonder the brain likes them so much. If you want to stretch, though, and explore a new idea, you've got to identify all of your assumptions associated with that idea and test every single one of them. The fact is, you don't know what you don't know, and testing can reveal to you what you don't know.

Testing isn't about trying on one hundred pairs of shoes to find the one pair that fits. You're not looking to confirm your assumptions, you're looking to determine their veracity and value in relation to your idea. You need to be as prepared to learn that an assumption is ridiculously flawed as to learn that it is valid. And then move on to the next assumption. You test and test and test . . . and sometimes you go so far as to flip the assumption, turning it on its head. This is the rigorous discovery stage of experimentation toward innovation.

Change Your Mindstate: M&M&M&M

It can be instructive to visualize how often (or not) you challenge your own assumptions and what you learn when you do.

Set up two jars and a bag of M&M'S. Label one jar ASSUMPTIONS and the other LEARNING. Every time you test an assumption, drop an M&M into the ASSUMPTIONS jar. After you test your assumption, drop as many M&M'S in the jar as things you learned from the experience. Then watch the jars fill up, especially the LEARNING jar.

Here's an example: I've got to go to the bank. I avoid using the drive-up window at my bank because I believe it's less convenient than going inside. I decide to test that assumption and pull up behind two cars in line for the drive-up window. I discover that using the drive-up window actually takes a few more minutes than going inside, but I also discover that while I wait in my car, I can make a quick call, listen to my music instead of the Muzak playing in the bank lobby, and continue enjoying the hot coffee I bought on my way to the bank. One M&M goes into the ASSUMPTIONS jar, three into the LEARNING jar. Ka-ching.

As you test, you take what you learn about what works, put it into practice, then test some more. That's what a batter is doing every time he steps up to the plate in baseball. Whether he strikes out, walks, or gets a hit, he's gathering information about the pitcher (what types of pitches he's throwing, how good the pitches are, etc.) that he will use to modify his approach in his next at-bat. Of course, the pitcher is also gathering information about the batter each time he comes to the plate (what kinds of pitches he's swinging at, how patient he is, etc.) that the pitcher uses to adapt his approach to that batter. Between the two of them, they go through seven or eight tests in a game—then do it all over again the next day.

Testing is essentially the taking of many small, frequent risks on the experimental road toward the future. It can be hard to take the first step, so make that one very doable. This lowers the barrier between just thinking about something and doing it. For example, my family had been talking for a while about how we might explore farming to feed ourselves more sustainably. Knowing this was an ambitious endeavor that might overwhelm or discourage us, we started by putting up a little greenhouse where we could all figure out what grows well together and when.

Taking a small first step like this creates immediate momentum. As you become more comfortable in the continuous testing mode, you'll find you are able to do it more quickly and more objectively. The learning that comes with every test should sharpen your idea, or transform it, or convince you to let it go, depending on what you learn.

Former Googler Jon Ratcliffe now runs a very "let's try it and see what happens" media company these days. "We probably run a hundred thousand experiments a year," he says. "For every video we create, we'll make a hundred iterations so we can play with all the variables. The developers spend hours and hours and thousands of dollars on these tests knowing that we'll learn valuable stuff we weren't expecting and can use in other ways. They have a lot of confidence in their own experimental process and this makes them nimble and resourceful."

If testing is the nerdy, brainy kid who was in your class at school, prototyping would be the jock/actor/jazz band kid—all performance. Prototyping is inherently more design oriented—it physically tests your vision of something, such as a product or a process. It lets you see what it might look like, how it would work (or not), and whether you like it enough to continue exploring.

Prototyping has a relationship with the old Silicon Valley mantra: "Fail fast." The idea being to use prototyping rapidly and repeatedly to identify flaws or weaknesses in a concept, or to prove that the concept has no value at all. But experimentation is not about failure, it's about learning. Prototyping helps you identify interesting ideas, explore them in a real, tangible way, and learn what can work right now and what can't. You don't fail fast, you learn fast.

I think of prototyping as a kind of ongoing conversation. You present your concept, gather immediate feedback, make adjustments, then present and discuss again. This goes on until the concept proves or disproves itself. Ultimately, if you want to put something out into the world, you want to begin a conversation about it right away so you can start to consider its myriad implications.

To introduce the essential nature of prototyping to our design students at Stanford, we hand them paper and Play-Doh and give them ten minutes to create a game. They usually come up with a couple of rules for the game, use the materials to convey the mechanics of the game, and maybe create a video that shows how to play the game. Through this very rudimentary prototyping, they can begin to understand their own assumptions and discover quickly what works and what's broken about their idea.

You have to keep thinking about what assumptions your prototype is testing and narrow down those assumptions to the one that feels most essential to the success of your idea—your LOF assumption. For example, you have an idea to radically expand the concept of "working from anywhere" with a floating desk in the sky. You think it's a hot idea, but you're not sure people would like working there. Prototyping this idea would help you quickly validate people's desire for such a thing and give you valuable information about how it should be designed. What is your LOF assumption? People like being up high, where there's a better view, as prices for hotel rooms and apartments are more expensive the higher they are. By identifying your central assumption, the prototype you put in the hands of users allows you to get the kind of specific feedback and real data you need to determine whether to move forward with your idea or to kill it.

Besides outing your assumptions, prototyping asks (and helps answer) two basic questions: Do people want this thing? And how should this thing work? When you create a prototype, you can either fake it or make it. Faking the functionality or appearance of the thing allows you to validate (or invalidate) it more quickly. Quickly, cheaply, or partially making the thing allows you to answer some fundamental questions about the design or the need it's attempting to address.

One of my students designed a quick and dirty experiment to attempt to solve a problem that was vexing her at work. On Google's Crittenden campus, it was hard to find meeting or videoconference rooms at certain critical times of the day. At the same time, many private offices were dead empty for big chunks of the day. Her idea was to create a simple, intuitive way for people to share their empty offices, kind of Airbnb-style (but free). Her LOF assumption was that office owners would be willing to share their space if it was easy to do.

She put small plastic sign holders outside of ten offices with a yellow IT'S COMING card in each holder. Then she left a pitch sheet on the office owners' desks that explained her idea and asked them to participate in her experiment. Next she replaced the yellow cards with green FREE/BUSY cards with space to indicate times the office was available. She quickly learned that only one office owner was unwilling to participate, and the other nine (and the many others in need of office space) were game from day one. This no-cost, high-learning prototype validated her assumption and paved the way for a more efficient and impactful use of office space.

To prototype your floating desk idea, you might put a desk on the roof of a high-rise building and get someone to work there for a week. You'll quickly learn it's windy up there. Also, the lack of amenities, such as a bathroom or a drinking fountain, is an issue, as is accessibility; however, the view was even more appealing to your user than you anticipated. Testing this idea with a quick fake-it prototype gave you enough information to refine your idea to test again.

Make-it prototyping requires somewhat of an investment of resources—time, materials, and usually a few willing participants. The idea is to spend as little as possible to gain a lot of information quickly to keep things moving along. At one point, the Google Glass development team considered enabling hand gesture controls. In about forty-five minutes, they built a prototype out of fishing line, hair bands, chopsticks, binder clips, and a whiteboard. This simple experiment taught them enough about the physical and social awkwardness of gesture-based navigation to bring a swift end to this product feature.

At the Stanford d.school, our mantra is "Prototype as if you're right and test as if you're wrong." Think of prototyping in terms of the questions it can answer for you and testing as a flaw detector. Together, they represent the power tools of experimentation.

Seek Risk

Some people have an appetite for risk, while others avoid it at all costs. If you fall in the latter category, you're going to need to build some chops for risk. I'm not talking about the free-falling-out-of-an-airplane kind of risk, more like the roll-the-dice kind of risk—but lots of it. Because experimentation is basically just an intelligent but continuous roll of the dice. So you not only need to get comfortable with risk, but you also gotta get good at it.

One of the easiest things to do to tune yourself up for risk is to shake up your daily routine. Start by making an exhaustive map of your day to identify every activity and behavior that is habitual. You will likely discover dozens of habits that guide your decisions and actions from the minute you wake up in the morning until you fall asleep at night. That's right, your habits own you.

Choose one item on that map, name five very different things you could do instead, and then do them, one day after the other. At first, you'll feel a little uncomfortable, even cranky, as you crave your usual routine. But each time, you will jog yourself a little further out of your groove and you'll begin to see and sense things about your experience you would not have noticed before.

My friends kid me about a habit I have—if you can call it that—of never going to a restaurant or hotel twice or taking the same route to get somewhere. Long ago, I decided it mattered more to me to discover something new every day than to become accustomed to anything. There's a little buzz that comes from not knowing what I'll encounter.

Having spent most of our lives oriented around clearly defined goals and success metrics, it can be unnerving to operate without them. One of my classes—"Designing with Radical Agency"—opens by presenting students with an empty syllabus and making clear they will be charting their own course to understanding the nature of agency. This freaks them out at first—What, no assignments? No grading rubric?—but eventually they find a way to navigate the ambiguity of the experience.

The idea is to leave behind the well-worn path. As pleasant and familiar as it may seem, it's really the enemy of discovery. Look for opportunities to engage in unplanned, open-ended experiences. Take a drive without a destination. Go somewhere—a museum, a new neighborhood, a park or garden—and get lost. Go on vacation with no plans, no must-dos. As you begin to acclimate to living in a state of uncertainty, you'll find you're more prepared and open to take risks and experiment.

Change Your Mindstate: Limb

Mountain climbers, aerialists, options traders—their every waking hour is defined by risk. They're not good at what they do because they can eliminate or control risk, they're good at it because they are able to confront risk head-on. To orient yourself toward the future, you have to get comfortable with the discomfort of risk. Identify a situation or an activity that you avoid doing because you aren't confident or fear an uncertain outcome. Now put yourself out on that limb. Does the thought of public speaking make you sweat? Seize the next chance you have to do a presentation. Do you hate talking about money? Pitch your boss for a raise. Are you shy around people you don't know? Go to a party and don't leave until you've had conversations with five strangers. Every time you come out the other end of a risk you've *chosen* to take, you become a bit more prepared for the unexpected risks the future is sure to present to you.

On March 25, 2013, at 1800 hours, I set sail from Punta Arenas for Patagonia—literally the end of the world—on the E-Ship (Entrepreneurship) with eighty young entrepreneurs, students, and professors from Stanford and the Pontificia Universidad Católica de Chile. Our mission was to use this time and the extraordinary experience to explore certain local creative challenges together, innovating our way toward solutions. During my class on experimentation, we were bedeviled by the roughest waves of the trip, which led to a considerable amount of seasickness (for me and many others), but also to some valuable lessons on testing, prototyping, and taking risks.

I observed something in Patagonia that made a deep impression on me. When a penguin jumps in the water, it faces a 50-percent chance of finding food and a 50-percent chance of being eaten by a predator. Yet there's always a lone penguin that jumps off the ice shelf into the water while the others watch who either comes back with food or dies trying. This is an act of extreme risk that provides critical information to the group, regardless of the outcome.

There are two aspects of this situation that intrigue me. First, the brave penguin doesn't just dip its flipper into the water to sort of see what might happen. It jumps in—all in—as if it believes it's going to return with a mouth full of fish. That's optimism. Second, if the first brave penguin meets an unfortunate end, another brave penguin will later step to the edge of the ice and jump in to gather new data. That's courage.

Every organization—and penguin colony—depends on the risktakers to venture into the unknown and come back with information that helps to light the path ahead for everyone else. I was so inspired by the brave penguins I saw in Patagonia that I created the Penguin Award at Google, which acknowledges a person who took a risk and helped other people learn something new. Penguin Award winners have undertaken an unconventional approach to a marketing campaign, adopted an untested approach to internal communications, and reimagined how to run a team meeting—every one of them a profile in corporate courage.

Artist and former Googler Seth Marbin discovered that taking risks can be liberating.

Right-Sizing Risk
SETH MARBIN

When I was a senior in high school, I went to Quito, Ecuador, as an exchange student. One day I hopped a bus headed for the jungle, a part of the country I hadn't explored yet. These buses are unusual in that when the bus slows down to approach a stop, people jump on and off while it's still moving. In the big cities, people often board with large packages of produce or handmade goods to sell at markets or take home to their villages. A helper throws their stuff on top of the bus while they jump on.

As we were traveling down a dirt road, I was sitting in a middle seat at the back of the bus when I realized I was starting to feel nauseous. It was hot and stuffy and packed with people, and I knew that if I didn't get off that bus I was going to be sick. But I couldn't get off because I knew the driver would leave me by the side of the road and drive away. I looked out the window and thought to myself, *What I need is fresh air. If I can make it to a window, I'll just climb out and go up to the top of the bus with the luggage.* So as the bus slowed down to pick up more people, I squeezed through the crowd to the closest window, crawled out, and pulled myself up onto the roof.

As I sat down amid the boxes and bags, I felt flushed with a sense of freedom. I was able to breathe and see the trees and the sky around me. What really stuck with me about this moment was learning that I had the power to change a situation that wasn't working for me and I could take steps to determine my own destiny. Ever since that day, I've felt sure that I can do something risky in a way that feels right to me. This has opened up so many possibilities in my life because I approach most situations believing that almost anything is changeable if I'm willing to take a risk. When I bump up against what look like fixed options or restrictive parameters, I say, "Why not?"

When I started working for Google in the area of search quality in 2006, the company had six thousand employees. One year later, there were twelve thousand employees. I spent a lot of time thinking about the potential impact this rapidly growing workforce could have in the communities where we worked. I discussed with many Googlers how they felt about all the resources and benefits we enjoyed as Google employees compared to what was happening in the world outside our Google bubble. I quickly learned that a lot of Googlers were interested in finding a way to drive some of their passion, problem-solving skills, and creative energy toward addressing challenges in the community. I thought, *Why not?*

Company leaders and managers encouraged me to see where this idea would go, so I recruited a team to pilot a community service initiative. The first year, three thousand people in thirty countries around the world volunteered with local organizations over the course of a week. With no budget and no dedicated staff in those first scrappy couple of years, we built an initiative that is now known as GoogleServe, an annual monthlong service opportunity that is available to the nearly two hundred thousand Googlers around the globe.

For the ten years I led GoogleServe, we approached it as an ongoing experiment where we prototyped, tested, and iterated repeatedly as we gathered more information about what worked and what greater impact might be possible. Early on, the culture at Google prioritized launching things quickly, but for this initiative, because so many of our community partners worked with vulnerable populations, we found we needed to take extra time to build relationships and evaluate the potential impacts on the community. It was important to regularly stop to think about whether we would actually be helping or harming the community and be mindful that wanting to "do good" didn't always have the intended outcome.

We were fueled by an optimism and vision of a future where service would be an integral part of our work culture and Googlers would see positive social impact as important as any other metric that drove our business.

First we tested what we call "hearts and hands" service—park cleanups or painting schools or planting trees. This was great for team building and had some value to our community partners. Then we started testing skills-based service (fixing a bug on a website, tutoring, or mentoring), which had a higher value because we were using skills not everyone has. Finally, we started offering pro bono service, which represented the application of our training and professional skills (e.g., legal, marketing, or engineering), as well as board service, the high-level strategic planning that a lot of nonprofits need but can't afford. As we got more involved in this kind of service, we were able to quantify the value to the communities where we volunteered.

I tend to think of everything as a draft, always subject to refinement. This lets me pause to empathize with the person or organization I'm working with and understand more about their challenges and factor in what I'm learning as I iterate. I also try to be careful not to always jump into problem-solving mode. Sometimes listening with empathy is just the support someone needs to identify their own solutions.

Separating intention from impact is also important. We used to send surveys to partner organizations after working with them, asking them whether the Googlers volunteering with them added value or helped advance the organization's mission. The surveys always came back with glowing responses. Then we realized a little skepticism might be in order. There's a power dynamic with any volunteers, in this case Google, the eight-hundred-pound gorilla, swooping in to help—who's going to tell us it was a bad experience? So we started testing different survey approaches that would allow the organization to share their impressions anonymously and give us more meaningful and actionable feedback.

During my time at Google, I was also able to test and iterate on my career by doing a little of what I wanted to be doing (leading volunteering and giving efforts) until that became my core job. By creating so much movement and data around volunteering and giving, I got to a place where my manager said, "Okay, write your own job description." This is what I meant about sitting on top of that bus and realizing I have a lot of power over what happens to me in the future.

I have a kind of backward planning process that's been helpful to me over the years. I start with the end in mind, a vision of a different world. So say I'm thinking of a world where there's a plate of freshly baked cookies in front of me. I haven't made them yet, but I can see them and smell them and totally taste them. Tapping as many senses as possible to put myself in that future state, I have a much better chance of achieving that vision. So instead of jumping into it and saying, "Okay, give me the recipe, I'm making some cookies," I take the time to practice anticipatory gratitude for this thing I've envisioned.

I don't know what's going to happen in the future. But I have so much control over the choices I make and how I act on those decisions. At Google, I learned that every choice I make can ripple out in a hundred directions. Today, thousands of Googlers participate in service projects that impact many thousands of people around the world, and some of them are even building this potential into products that millions of people may use.

Turn the Page

It's exciting to see someone filled with passion about a new idea. It's like they're in the early days of a romantic relationship—everything about it is intoxicating, exciting, all-consuming. But what if the idea is actually like that one regrettable fling you had in college—just a really bad match that made your friends look at you funny until it blew over? It can be hard to know you're in a wrong relationship when you want so badly for it to work.

You should just quit trying something that doesn't work, right? Sounds obvious, but you'd be surprised how many people just keep trying the same approach even when it has proven to be ineffective. This is often the result of testing an assumption you stubbornly believe to be true, so much so that you can't see that it's actually a bum assumption.

People often fall in love with their own ideas and as a result find it difficult to let them go when experimentation proves that they're not viable. This emotional attachment is not constructive. That test we do at the start and end of every semester at the Stanford d.school reveals an additional benefit that comes from getting good at experimentation. Testing, getting early feedback, learning from it, and quickly testing again grows the students' confidence to move on when something doesn't work. They become more invested in the process than in some ideal outcome and as a result, they avoid clinging to an idea that's not panning out. This may be the single most valuable skill they take away from the class.

At Google X, we came to realize the extreme value of letting go when it comes to innovation. To get people to stop working on a project that wasn't delivering the desired results, we incentivized people to let go by giving them extra vacation days, a bonus, and a guarantee that they'd work on a future X project. At first, just one person raised their hand to drop their project, but others followed soon after. It was kind of magical, seeing people walk away from one thing they had become attached to so they could focus on something new and different. Acknowledge what you have learned from every idea and experiment and then move on.

You've seen those ancient nautical maps in history books, the ones that feature monsters at the edges to depict the dangerous, don't-go-there places. The monsters did a great job of keeping travelers from going anywhere near the unknown. What if instead those maps showed treasure and bounty to suggest what might be found beyond the horizon? I guarantee those seamen would have discovered the New World and a whole bunch of other stuff a lot faster if they thought those places represented possibility rather than peril.

Experimentation propels you right to that same edge of the unknown. You can see that there's opportunity there if you're in the right frame of mind to do something about it. Being mentally prepared to experiment and test solutions immediately and continuously means you can actually try out your future today.

Do you

test

each

OPPOR-

TUNI-

TY?

Try This

After you read this, close your eyes.

Visualize the people on planet Earth
who came before you.

How did they help you?

How did they negatively impact you?

Visualize the people on planet Earth
who will come after you?

How could you help them?

How could you negatively impact them?

CHAPTER 6

Expansive Empathy

Expansive empathy connects one human experience to another. These are the intersections you create and the bridges you build on the path toward your future.

When a person goes on a silent meditation retreat, it's reasonable for them to expect silence, right?

The ten-day retreat I attended in December 2021 was an intense experience. For ten hours a day, I sat in silence with forty-nine other meditators on floor cushions in an open room without much distance between us. For the first couple of days, I was very conscious of what "silence" in this room sounded like: I could hear my own breathing, of course, but also the breathing of the four people sitting closest to me and maybe the occasional cough from somewhere else in the room.

As I became accustomed to these sounds, I was able to focus on being more fully aware of my own breath and physical sensations and learning not to judge my observations. I was beginning to feel a different connection to my mind and body. On the morning of day six, I noticed that the person taking the seat behind me was unwrapping one of the cough drops that were available outside of the meditation hall. I quickly became aware of (okay, obsessed with) the sound of him sucking on the cough drop and turning it over and over in his mouth. By the time we took a break, I was a bit of a wreck. Not only had I not focused on my own practice that morning, but I'd spent the entire time disparaging this guy in my head. Believe me, this is not what you want to see at a meditation retreat.

After the break, he sat in the same spot behind me and spent an hour sucking on another cough drop. I spent the hour desperately mulling how to get him to stop. Should I talk to him? Not allowed at a silent retreat! Should I write him a note? Also not allowed. Should I hide all the cough drops? Maybe . . .

The next morning, it started all over again. But over the course of the day, I managed to bring my attention back to my own meditation practice by trying to observe myself and this gentleman without judgment. I started thinking about what he might be experiencing, whether he might be a kind, responsible person just trying to avoid coughing out of courtesy to the other meditators in the room. In a moment, my agitation turned to a compassion that kind of washed over me. Now I wanted to thank him for giving me an opportunity to not just understand empathy but to really experience that change in perspective, maybe for the first time.

Anyone can have a moment of empathy, as I did with the cough drops guy, where you are suddenly able see something from their perspective and it shifts your own perspective. Those moments are remarkable.

Picture this happening in a grocery store parking lot: It's raining hard, and a man is rushing to his car carrying a paper bag full of groceries when the bag splits open. He freezes in the middle of the road, helplessly clutching his stuff to his chest to keep it from spilling onto the pavement. Out of nowhere, a woman appears in front of him with a big plastic FreshDirect bag she uses to catch everything he has in his arms except for a couple of oranges that drop and roll away.

The woman was loading her own purchases into the trunk of her car when she saw his dilemma and jumped to his aid. Thanking her over and over again, he takes his groceries to his car and runs back to return the bag to her. Here is the part I like best about this ninety-second scene: she waves him off and says, "Keep the bag. You'll do the same for someone else one day."

At a glance, this incident might seem like just a case of one person showing another person a bit of kindness. It is that, but it's also so much more. Look a little closer:

The woman sees what's happening and doesn't look away.

She immediately connects with how the man is feeling in that miserable moment.

She instinctively acts because she recognizes those feelings.

Both of their perspectives shift during this brief exchange.

Finally, this story is not over—other things will happen to these people as a result of this experience.

This is **expansive empathy**. It's rational, responsive, and transformative. It reverberates. And it hinges on our humanity. Unlike the other dimensions of a future-ready mindstate, this one only exists and is exercised in relation to another human being.

Humans possess a self-awareness that distinguishes us from other species.[1] We also have an innate selfishness that can cause us not to see or hear another member of our species who is standing right in front of us. I promise this is not the case for the rest of the animal kingdom. This is a blind spot we live with to some degree for our entire lives. Only empathy can truly take us out of ourselves and into the community of others.

Confucian philosophy describes empathy using the word "Ren," meaning "two persons," or "co-humanity." Aristotle also connected the concept of empathy with our humanity, essentially defining it as having an understanding of one another that enables us to know what it means to be human. But what difference does it make if I know "what it means to be human"?

The short answer is because you're more likely to survive in this world if you understand your cohabitants. Further, when you understand them, you develop a better understanding of yourself, which increases your chances of also having a meaningful, rewarding life. I think that the Confucian notion of "co-humanity" gets right to the heart of it—we're on this planet together. If relating to one another humanely—thinking of another person's needs along with our own—can preserve and also enrich our lives, why wouldn't we do that?

For our future-ready purposes, the better question is: What difference will exercising empathy make to my future?

Unless you plan to spend the rest of your life alone on a remote island, you need to believe that empathy is crucial to building the future you want on a planet where there are billions of other people trying to do some version of the same thing. You will not succeed in getting what you want if you aren't also thinking about what all of your co-humans want. Imagine you're the sleep-deprived parent of a newborn baby. For the moment, all you want your future to consist of is one full night of uninterrupted sleep. Until you are able to understand that baby's wants and needs, you are not having that future. Empathy isn't a moral imperative, it's a practical one.

You intersect with dozens of people (or more) every day. Most of those intersections are silent and invisible, but each of them is an opportunity for you to acknowledge your shared humanity with those people. In some instances, you may recognize a stranger's feelings, as the woman in the parking lot did. In others, you may make an empathetic connection with someone you know—a colleague, a casual acquaintance, or a friend or family member. I think of every one of those intersections as a tiny spark that may light something in me or in the other person that contributes to a better outcome in that moment, that day, or even over a lifetime.

To be clear, empathy isn't selflessness. It's not even necessarily altruistic. To sacrifice your own self-interest in favor of someone else's—well, your ego generally doesn't want you to do that. But when your empathy produces a good-for-me/good-for-you outcome, it proves that it's possible to balance your motivation to meet your own needs with the consideration of the needs of others.

You may never know whether your empathy for someone else changed anything or made things better for that person, but you will learn that it *always* changes and benefits *you*. And once you have experienced this for yourself, you'll find you will choose to tap your empathy because it's actually a pretty good deal for you.[2]

As with the other dimensions of the future-ready mindstate, when you act more frequently and consistently with this dimension engaged—as your empathy expands—the choices you have in front of you multiply and get more interesting and surprising. Your choices also become more human-focused and impactful for yourself and others. Empathy sharpens your understanding of what you want the future to be, as social entrepreneur and ex-Googler Sandra Camacho's work vividly illustrates.

Seeing Things in a New Light

SANDRA CAMACHO

I started working at Google right out of college. The fast-paced environment was intense at first, but I quickly embraced the Google philosophy of learning, persevering, and experimenting. A few years in, I joined Frederik's CSI:Lab community and began a series of experiments in pursuit of my passion for design and the human experience. These experiments ultimately led me to an important realization: I needed to mold my career around my own interests, not around the interests of an organization or a particular role.

After eight years, I left Google to launch my own business as an inclusive design strategist and educator. In this role, I work with values-driven organizations and people to address inequity, bias, and exclusion in the design process. I guide them through the culture, mindset, and workflow shifts necessary to design for more inclusive and equitable outcomes. This means looking in the mirror to identify your own biases and assumptions and zooming out to discern systemic barriers to inclusion and equity.

For example, I once did a boot camp for a design consulting firm on the subject of intersectional design. Given that both designers and "traditional" consultants would be attending, I wanted the conversation to be based in reality rather than theory. I started the session with a couple of games to help participants gain awareness of their own privilege. Then I brought in a user panel made up of people from marginalized groups who represented a genuine multiplicity of perspectives. I centered the discussion entirely around the panelists' own voices and stories without allowing the audience to ask questions as they would normally expect to do. I wanted to demonstrate how the panelists could hold the power of their own narrative when an interviewer's power was removed from the equation.

After hearing the panelists' stories, the participants split into teams to do a "Black Mirror" type of exercise to imagine the potential harm and unintended consequences that may result from the design of a digital health technology that could disproportionately affect marginalized groups. The participants identified data privacy concerns for sensitive health information and the inaccessibility of the platform for disabled patients or those without suitable devices. Direct engagement with marginalized groups puts you right in the middle of lived experiences that are often overlooked or minimized in the design process. It allows you to anticipate and preempt potential harm on marginalized communities and better serve their needs based on deep understanding rather than unvalidated assumptions and bias.

A few months later, I spoke to a designer who had attended this workshop and she told me this exercise made her think about empathy in a whole new light. She was excited to share that her firm had created a stress test to use during prototyping to check their designs against possible harm to users, especially people in the margins of society.

In another instance, I spent six months working with the Paris-based team from Libraries Without Borders, a global NGO that connects people to books and digital resources in under-resourced communities and post-emergency situations. I joined the NGO to support them in the design of services and experiences for vulnerable populations who have little or no access to culture and information. This group had worked with the famous French designer Philippe Stark to create the Ideas Box, a colorful, mobile pop-up multimedia center to take into refugee camps and emergency shelters. I hoped to help them better understand the needs of displaced populations and create more inclusive, user-centric experiences for them.

When I saw that a survey they used to assess learning needs of residents in the emergency shelters was filled with biased, leading questions, I said, "Hey, let's go meet the residents and do some user interviews." I wanted them to try to understand the residents' life journeys on a deeper level rather than just collecting lists of books and cultural content that interested them. I was surprised by how resistant this team was to my suggestion. They were mostly young people who were enthusiastic about what they were doing, but they didn't appreciate my disrupting the way they work.

To address this resistance to change, I had to shift the focus away from transforming processes and toward transforming their perspective. This meant training the team on the value and relevance of experience design for vulnerable populations. We did exercises focused on storyboarding and customer journey mapping that put them in front of real people. This obliged them to gain a more empathetic understanding of the lived experiences of these refugees and asylum seekers. The team had a pretty fixed sense of their top-down operating model—they saw themselves as an NGO bringing a service to these shelters rather than imagining what residents of the shelters have experienced and how an educational service might aid them in achieving their goals.

The team's resistance made this a tough project for me, and I wasn't sure we were making any progress. But by the end of our time together I could see they were starting to rethink their perspective and the tools and processes that they had previously taken for granted. The most rigid and oppositional person on this team later told me that it was surprising for them to realize that they weren't really centering on users as much as they thought they were. This confirmed to me that a real perspective shift was happening.

This is the place I have carved out for myself in the design field: helping design practitioners understand the value of designing for equity and inclusion and for marginalized communities. It's not always a comfortable place to be. Openly addressing topics such as social justice, privilege, or power imbalances can feel disruptive and can come into conflict with the goals and norms of capitalism and "business as usual." But this work is incredibly valuable. It has considerable social and business benefits and amplifies positive impact and reduces societal harm while fueling innovation and extending the reach of solutions we design.

I believe I'm playing a role in redefining empathy in the design world. People and organizations often believe they're practicing empathy by expressing "we care" or "we can help make it better" through what they're doing but there's an inherent elitism, a kind of "we know better" posture, that is really the opposite of empathy. It's "we" centered, not "you" centered. Authentic empathy is a lot about keeping yourself in check from projecting your life experience onto someone else. At heart, it's endless, tireless, critical reflection.

Practicing expansive empathy is an ongoing exercise in shifting your perspective from "I" to "you," seeking information you don't have, and trying to anticipate the consequences of what might happen.

From First Person to Second Person

When I'm preparing for a speaking engagement, I focus on refining the ideas I want to share and the questions I want the audience to take away from my talk. Just before I step onto the stage, however, I take a moment to look at the people in the audience and think about where each of them may be in their lives. I do this to remind myself that the most important factor in the chemistry of the event and the outcome of our exchange is them, not me.

When your name and picture are on the big screen behind you and all the eyes in the room are fixed on you, it's easy to misunderstand this. In reality, no matter what my intention is, the potential for impact rests entirely inside each of the people in the audience. I can't know what they're feeling or what they may be going through on that day. But I do know that any hope I have to spark a connection with them is directly related to their unique feelings and state of mind in that moment.

To get to this place where empathy lives—at the slightest juncture of "I" and "you"—start by putting your own history and worldview in the back seat. Yes, those things are an important part of you, but they tend to dominate your perspective and make you project your experience onto the other person, which is missing the point altogether.

How do you quiet the first person (I) so you can gain an understanding of the second person (you)? *Stop talking.* Seriously, just hold your tongue. You don't need to articulate all the thoughts you're having about what you believe or how you feel or what happened to you. As meaningful as those thoughts may be to you, none of them will help you see another person or appreciate their experience.

Shockingly, when you talk less, you can *listen harder* and *notice more.* You can hear everything the other person is saying, not just the little bits and pieces that manage to get past all the words coming out of your mouth. And you can really feel the difference between just hearing and really listening. You start to notice *all* of the information the person is conveying through their vocabulary and tone and facial expressions and body language. You'll even notice what they're not saying, which can be a critical clue to what they're actually feeling or going through.

Change Your Mindstate: Mirror

Sometimes when you're walking down the street and catch your reflection in a window, you see something different, something else about yourself. This experiment helps you capture a little more of that something else. It also lets you see yourself as others might see you and ultimately regard other people more fully and less critically. Do it alone and in a quiet place.

Stand in front of a mirror, preferably a full-length mirror so you can see your entire body. Take a photo of your reflection in the mirror. Now observe yourself as a whole for a few minutes. Try to be neutral as you look at yourself, avoiding judgment about what you see.

Next focus on different parts of you, starting at the top of your head and slowly moving down to your feet. Look at your hands. Do they say anything about your life story and the experiences that have shaped the person in the mirror? Can you see any of the joy or pain you have felt in your life on your face?

Now think about your image as if it is a portrait in an art gallery. What might someone looking at your portrait be able to discern about you? What assumptions might they make based on your expression or your posture or how you're dressed? They couldn't know you, of course, but they would be looking for something in you that they can relate to. What does this portrait offer to that stranger?

Do this exercise again on another day. Maybe position yourself sitting instead of standing or standing but turned slightly in profile. Later compare the two photos. You will see something different this time because you *are* different. Maybe you're more rested or feeling more stress than you did before. Or maybe you're different because you've changed the way you look at yourself and others.

Some years back, I was staying with friends in Berlin and one of them invited me to visit a Syrian refugee camp where she was working. I eagerly accepted. The night before I was to join her at the camp, I lay awake coming up with all these ideas for helping the hundreds of people arriving there every day. I narrowed my ideas down to a handful of really solid ones that I was certain would work, then slept like a saint thinking about all the good I was going to do the next day.

Soon after I arrived at the camp, I realized that my schemes for collecting food and toys and clothing for the refugees were not going to be helpful at all. Massive piles of these items had already been donated and were sorted and ready to be distributed. I was so disappointed in myself for forgetting my own principle of empathy. This happens all the time in our work. In the rush to get that great product out the door or a slick new service launched, we forget how important it is to hear from the customer what they want or need. Then we're crushed when the product or service fails to catch on.

It wasn't too late for me to observe and listen carefully to some of these people tell their stories. The newly arrived refugees were only stopping over at the camp for one night. The next day, they would have to go to another location to register with the government so they could begin to establish a legal presence in the country. Then they would be assigned to another camp that would be their base until they settled in the country. They had left Syria in a hurry, many of them carrying their belongings in a makeshift parcel. A very simple need they had—and obvious, once I opened my eyes and ears—was a backpack or rolling suitcase to carry their possessions with them as they moved from place to place.

These folks needed a hammer while I'd been trying to push a wrench into their hands. You have to get out of your own head and away from what you think you know to get even a glimpse of the truth of someone else's experience. Going from the perspective of the first person to understanding the perspective of the second person is a constant but continuously enlightening effort. All you can do is keep trying to put your own perspective aside so you can learn something about the other person, perhaps something that connects you in a way that touches or changes you both.

Fill in the Gaps

You will never quite achieve knowing another person's experience, even with someone you feel close to. When you know someone well enough that you find yourself assuming something about their feelings or experience, you should stop yourself right there. There is no assumption you could make that is fully and completely accurate. In fact, I can promise you that whatever you think you know is full of surprising holes.

A friend once described a complicated project she led that was going to culminate in a high-stakes client presentation. There were all kinds of people involved—in-house staff from multiple departments, outside consultants and subject matter experts, technical writers, and designers. Jillions of moving parts, she said, describing the difficulty in pulling together the many components of the project.

After two months of intensive work and less than a week out from the client meeting, the guy responsible for taking all the content the group had developed and turning it into a knock-your-socks-off deck sent an email to the group that said, "I'm sorry but I will be unable to complete this presentation." My friend then had to scramble to find someone who could step in and finish the work.

She said at the time she'd been too crazed and anxious just getting the presentation finished to think much about the guy who dropped out of the project. After the client meeting was over, though, she got good and mad about the difficult spot he'd put her in. Unreliable! Unprofessional! Inconsiderate!

A year or so later, his name came up during a launch meeting for another project. Someone was suggesting he would be good to engage to work on the final deck. Before my friend could launch into the scorching assessment of the man that she'd been rehearsing in her head for months, another person chimed in. "He's such a talented guy. It's great he's working again after that awful car accident."

Ouch. All this while she'd been harboring a fiercely negative impression of him because he had inconvenienced her. She never once thought to reach out to him and learn what actually happened. Further, she'd allowed this information vacuum to become filled with her own misguided misanthropy—and she came *this close* to making things worse for a guy who had clearly been through a lot.

Ignorance has a lot of power to impede and distort your understanding of another person's experience. To have a clearer, more accurate understanding, you have to fill in the gaps of your knowledge. But if you don't know what you don't know, how do you discover the information you don't have?

Ask yourself: *What am I missing? What could I be unaware of that might make this picture more complete?* My friend could have just messaged the man on her project team, "Hey, what's up?" to fill in the gaps in her knowledge. Or she could have started by asking herself, "What could possibly make me walk away from an important project the way he did?" Either approach would have presented her with different, more constructive choices in the way she reacted to what happened.

It can be humbling—even shocking—when you learn something new that changes your whole perception of a person's situation. You think, *Oh, I don't really know anything at all!* But this is actually where the most important learning begins. Your openness and curiosity will lead you to new information that adds detail to the picture. You take yourself for a long walk in the other person's shoes to closely consider different aspects of their experience. As the picture gets clearer, what the information means to you and what you might do with it also becomes clearer. More information, more dots, more choices.

Change Your Mindstate: Switch

Attempting to explain someone else's point of view can be uniquely illuminating to you and the other person. This experiment has you switching positions with someone else to better understand why they think the way they do.

Say you and a friend have different views on a subject that is important to both of you. Maybe it's kids and homework or adults working from home. You have discussed this issue a number of times so you're familiar with each other's position. Give yourselves two minutes each to explain the other person's thinking as if it's your own.

You're wearing your friend's shoes now and maybe they're a bit uncomfortable. But as you search for the right way to convey what *you* think *they* think, you find yourself trying to make careful word choices. When you're just listening to your friend talk about this subject, it's easy to simplify or generalize as you process what they say. When you're trying to express it yourself, you realize there's depth and nuance to their position because it comes from their personal experience. And hearing your position described by another person makes you look at how you express yourself in a different light.

This is extra interesting to do in a small group of people who know each other well but have different opinions on a subject. Everyone walks away with an expanded appreciation for each other's perspectives.

Former Googler Laura Jones describes a program she ran at Uber that put employees in the driver's seat of an Uber car. Using the driver's technology, the employee would gain an end-to-end understanding of the driver's job, particularly specific pain points. Over time, the employee driving program helped Laura see an opportunity to reward the drivers who were doing the most driving with Uber. Her first inclination was to offer an education benefit, along the lines of the popular programs Walmart and Starbucks provide their employees.

But what information was Laura missing? Her team met face-to-face with Uber drivers around the world and discovered that the majority of tenured drivers in most countries were middle-aged men, often immigrants who said they drove for Uber to make better lives for their families. As Laura and her team got to know the people behind the wheel, she realized that the education benefit she had in mind might not be as useful to these drivers as she had anticipated. But recognizing the hopes they had for their families, she recommended that the benefit be giftable to anyone in the driver's family. Making the effort to learn more about these drivers gave her better options to design a program that spoke to their unique aspirations and experience.

In the end, you fill in the most important gaps when you begin to understand what motivates someone else to say or do what they do. A keynote I did for the Federal Bureau of Investigation in Washington, DC, brought this fact home for me from an unexpected angle.

Like a lot of organizations, the FBI feels pressure to get ahead of the curve of change. They asked me to talk to them about how the agency might think about the future to strengthen its position today. I walked about 150 leaders and employees from across the agency through the dimensions of a future-ready mindstate, with a particular focus on tapping empathy to think like the user of a product or service to stimulate innovation.

I explained that when you try to see an experience through the eyes of a user, what's missing in your understanding of the user becomes instantly apparent. Here's a good example of this: When YouTube launched its video upload app for iOS, developers quickly noticed that around 10 percent of the videos that users had uploaded were upside down. After a close look at why this was happening, they learned that these users weren't filming or uploading their videos incorrectly; they were rotating their phones 180 degrees *the way left-handed people tend to do*. The developers had inadvertently designed an app for themselves, a bunch of righties.

The FBI audience was very interested in this subject, perhaps because they think about what they know and don't know about the "user" all the time. Whether they're involved in a crisis negotiation or tracking the movements of a cybercriminal, they're focused on having a keen understanding of the individual's circumstances, motives, and feelings. Formally trained in what they call "tactical empathy," they seemed pretty highly evolved on the empathy scale. And they reminded me that I don't have to agree with or like someone to empathize with them. I just need to set aside my own feelings and judgment and pay very close attention to try to understand how that person sees the world.

Sometimes, the best way to get closer to understanding the underlying feelings or experiences behind someone's behavior or point of view is to just ask "Why?" Twisting a little on the "5 Whys" method for determining the root cause of a problem (repeatedly asking "why" until you land on the real reason the problem occurred), allow yourself three "whys" to fill in the gaps about something you don't know about another person.

Example: You've never given any thought to the fact that your friend doesn't like dogs, but today you ask her, "Why don't you like dogs?" She says, "They're scary." You ask her, "Why are they scary?" She says, "They bite." You ask her, "Why do you think they bite?" She says, "When I was a kid, I was walking home from school one day and a dog jumped out of the bushes and attacked me. I had to go to the emergency room and get stitches where he bit me on the leg."

Wow. You just went from having no information on this subject to having a vivid picture of something fairly traumatic that happened to your friend as a child. You didn't just get an answer to an idle question on an innocuous subject—you learned something that gives you a deeper, more nuanced understanding of her.

Consider the Consequences

We practice empathy when we attempt to understand where some-one's coming from—their personal history and the experiences they've had that make them see the world as they do. But what if it's not possible to learn these things about another person? How can empathy influence your choices in the absence of specific informa-tion about someone else's experience or perspective?

Practice predictive empathy by orienting your thinking around what you already know about human nature. What makes people scared? What makes them laugh? What makes them worry? What makes them feel lonely or hopeful or frustrated? You have some pretty accurate answers to those questions because as a human being you've been there before—you have felt all these emotions and you have a good idea from your own experience where they come from. And this rich body of knowledge you already possess offers you an infinite number of choices about what to do with it.

Predictive empathy simply requires us to be consciously human. Admittedly, we don't always walk around thinking about our hu-manity. In fact, it's weird how easy it is to not think about it at all when we're out doing errands or walking the dog or running to catch a train. The taskier our lives become, the less thought we give to our humanity. It's like gravity—we know it's there, but it doesn't need us to think about it to be true.

It's your humanity that causes you to be creative and collaborative and resourceful. If you're tuned in to your humanity, it's like you're looking through a kaleidoscope seeing potential in every shape and color. When you become too detached from your humanity, the shapes and colors fade and you start running out of ideas and solutions.

One of the principles of design thinking that helps to draw you back the idea of humanity is human-centered design. Design thinking focuses on creating products or processes that respond specifically to human needs. Designers look closely at a user's motivation and behavior when conceptualizing, then move through stages of prototyping and experimentation that incorporate user feedback to adjust and refine. Paying careful attention to the user's slightest responses gives designers information that allows them to solve for the user's latent, unarticulated, and unmet needs.

Human-centered design asks the question: What specific implications would my product or service have on a human being? And what are the implications for a community of humans? The human-centered approach naturally expands to encompass "life-centered" considerations of environmental and social implications—we should try to ensure that what benefits the individual also benefits society as a whole, or at least does no harm.

I believe that anything and everything can be evaluated in terms of its human-centeredness. When my son was small, I hung a mobile of brightly colored cars and trucks over his bed. Given the amount of time he spent lying there staring up at the mobile, I was surprised he wasn't showing more interest in things that go vroom. One day, I happened to lie down on the floor next to his bed and look up at the mobile. Instead of cars and trucks, I saw thin slivers of cardboard that were more confusing than comforting.

I was so glad to catch this glimpse of my son's perspective. It made me realize how often we blindly accept conventional wisdom or our own ideas and assumptions about the needs of a child because they aren't able to explicitly express those needs themselves.

Older people are often in the same boat. Many of the choices and activities associated with the end stages of life are not at all human centered. The individual experiencing this phase tends to become the passenger instead of the driver, with decisions made on their behalf by people who lack information about what the human at the center of all this might really want or need.

If the end of life was a product, how would you think about developing a human-centric design for it?

Your "user" is the individual—a human being—who is dying. Keeping their preferences and challenges in mind, you engage the user to assess their needs in relation to all of the people involved in this experience, the environment where the experience will take place, and the process that determines how and what decisions are made that impact this user.

You could break down this evaluation into dozens of components within these three categories of information, each piece giving you more human-centric data you can use to shape a desirable and achievable experience for this user. Instead of getting what the medical field or religious institutions or the funerary industry thinks this user should experience, they get something that makes sense to them and suits their human wants and needs.

When you hone your lens of human-centeredness, you see that opportunities for better are everywhere. And you get more adept at anticipating and acting on these opportunities quickly and confidently. For Googler Astrid Weber, empathy has shaped her unique path as a UX designer and global change maker.

Building Community Through Empathy

ASTRID WEBER

Since I was a child I've been driven by openness to new experiences and my curiosity about what the universe holds in store for us. I joined Google straight out of my master's program at the University of the Arts in Berlin, Germany. My first 20 percent project was teaching design thinking with Frederik's CSI:Lab community. My core work at Google has been diverse, from building the first version of Google Calendar on Android to defining the User Experience (UX) standards for accessibility to working on refugee and climate tech projects with Google.org.

I need a great sense of stimulation to feel like I'm making the most of my time in this world. When you constantly place yourself in different situations and meet new people, you become more aware of who you are and how the world works. I am always working toward a deeper knowledge of myself and a more intimate understanding of my own needs, which entails trying just as hard to understand who other people are and what they need.

I don't just try to imagine what a situation might be like. I actively put myself in lots of situations with an awareness of and openness to different perspectives I encounter everywhere I go. Professionally, I'm a UX practitioner. Personally, I find that empathy—my interest in exposing myself to and understanding other perspectives—kind of pushes me toward the work I want to do next. This has made my career trajectory look a little different from someone who makes the traditional moves to advance within an organization.

For example, I've collaborated on the development of an open-source CO_2 calculator with a start-up in Sweden that is working on climate change. I've organized and led teams on refugee response projects for the International Rescue Committee in Jordan, Greece, Serbia, and Tunisia. When the war on Ukraine started, I helped kick-start a Google collaboration with an activist-led NGO there. After the support site was established, I helped put a team of Google volunteers in place to advance and scale the operation. Now I serve on the board of directors of the NGO and advise them on strategy and technology.

I frequently need to drop into the middle of a new situation, figure out what needs to happen, work out a process, then teach other people how to take it from there. I push the people I've trained forward to do the job right away. I like to build communities where people aren't acting like lone wolves but instead are inspiring and empowering one another to do their best work. In my early years at Google, the spirit was very much about trusting people to do what's right and learn what they need to learn along the way. It was like, "Hey, we hired you. We believe you'll do a good job. Now go do it." I got a lot of confidence working in this environment because I wasn't learning by observing, I was learning by doing. This is how I have progressed and grown through every stage of my career, by diving right into each learning opportunity with a healthy disrespect for the impossible.

Similar considerations guide my thinking when I'm building a team these days. Normally you're supposed to hire based on experience. You scan a candidate's CV and have confidence in their abilities because of the schools they attended or the companies they worked for. But I never hire based on those factors alone. I hire smart people who have passion and want to grow. I've brought on people with little UX experience—among them architects and computer game developers—and they have developed into some of the strongest UX researchers I know.

I find that people who seek to learn and grow are wide open to feedback and naturally expose themselves to new situations. Working with them becomes a lively back-and-forth, where they take the bits of input or vision that I share, make it their own, then come back again and again as the project takes shape. This is where it gets really interesting because now it's like we're dancing. The work gets stronger with each exchange as our different perspectives help inspire ideas that neither of us had at the beginning of the project.

Empathy is about being human together. It's about seeking community, not isolating yourself within your microcosms but instead acknowledging that you need one another, that you need to understand and involve others if you want to make good things happen. Ultimately, empathy is the source of positive change.

On the eve of an annual gathering of leaders and strategic partners of the family-owned Faber-Castell company in Stein, Germany, I had dinner with Countess Mary von Faber-Castell, the family matriarch, and her daughter Countess Katharina von Faber-Castell. I had been invited by Katharina to attend this meeting and begin work with the company on a number of innovation initiatives. The meeting was to take place in the family's very old castle, which intrigued me, I admit.

For three centuries, Faber-Castell has produced expensive, high-quality pencils, pens, art supplies, and stationery that are sold around the world. Founded in 1761, the company has survived the Industrial Revolution and multiple wars and has adapted well to the rapid modernization of commerce in the digital age. In the years Faber-Castell was led by Katharina's late father, Count Anton-Wolfgang von Faber-Castell, the company became a premium global brand and a pioneering advocate for sustainability and corporate environmental responsibility.

By all accounts, Faber-Castell was in solid shape. But Katharina expressed concerns to me about whether the company's leadership and eight thousand worldwide employees had the vision or capability to navigate the future. She was just being realistic—she wondered whether ten years from now a manufacturer of pencils and pens would have something relevant to offer a generation of consumers who hold devices in their hands?

This was one of the most interesting projects I had ever worked on. It had it all: a fascinating old company and family, a compelling business story, beautiful products, and a shrinking consumer base. I was confident I could help them find their own approach to innovation, but I discovered right away that I had a more immediate challenge: understanding the distinct perspectives of the colorful and complicated cast of characters at the helm of this company.

After months of conversations with each of them, here's the short version of what I learned:

Countess Mary cared about preserving the traditions, history, and status of the company—change wasn't what she was looking for. Countess Katharina was energetic and future-thinking but struggled to convince others of the urgent need to adopt new approaches. Katharina's brother, Count Charles, was intent on taking over the leadership of the company. Then-CEO Daniel Rogger was focused on his responsibility to run the company. And Katharina's younger sisters, Countesses Victoria and Sarah, were contemplating their own careers.

Each of these people wanted the company to continue to succeed. But family businesses are notoriously complex, and there was no chance of helping this group to align their interests. The effort it took to understand their unique motivations enabled me to show them how supporting innovation would advance their individual agendas.

With their cooperation, we launched an internal innovation coaching community to provide training to individuals across the organization. We also created new mission, vision, and values statements to express a future-facing position for the company. We didn't answer Katharina's question about what Faber-Castell would have to offer the world in the future. But I think we considered the better question: Will we be ready for whatever opportunity or challenge the future might bring?

Change Your Mindstate: Note

This experiment can happen whenever you're out and around other people—for example, while you're sitting in a waiting room, standing in a line, riding public transportation, or waiting for a meeting to start. Identify a person in your line of sight. It's best if the person is a stranger because it helps you minimize your assumptions and focus on your observations and predictions. And be careful not to be observed observing—in other words, don't stare and mind your manners.

Observe: Look closely at the person and observe their appearance, facial expressions, body language, behavior, and interactions with their surroundings. Be conscious of not judging them or invading their privacy.

Empathize: Imagine what they might be thinking or feeling in the moment you're observing them. Consider what their current mood might be.

Predict: Based on your observations, predict how they might react to a simple potential scenario. For example, how might they behave if someone calls their name or it suddenly starts to rain? The scenario can be anything that's plausible in the context of the setting.

Reflect: Notice what the person does in response to what happens to them while you're watching. Was your prediction of their reaction close to what you expected? Or were you surprised by their reaction?

Repeat: Do this exercise whenever you find yourself in a situation such as this. The more you do it, the more observant and attuned to another person's emotional state and behavior you will become.

Using predictive empathy to consider specific possibilities when asking that question stimulates the imagination and creative response. In an innovation training that I conducted many times at Google, we worked with a "futures wheel," which is a visual tool used in scenario planning to explore the direct and indirect future implications of any given event or trend. We'd start by identifying what we want to consider and writing it in the center of a whiteboard—let's say our subject is self-driving cars.

Then we would identify the first-order consequences of the presence of self-driving cars in day-to-day life. We ask ourselves: What will likely happen as the immediate result of this? Probably fewer accidents, less government revenue from traffic violation fines, more cars on the roads. We'd note all of those results and connect them with lines to "self-driving car" at the center of the board.

Next we would ask ourselves: What will happen when each of these first-order consequences happens? Fewer car repairs, fewer driving fatalities, more cost to maintain the more heavily trafficked roads. We'd note these second-order consequences and connect them to the first-order consequences with lines. We would continue with this process for as many levels of consequences as are relevant and useful to fully imagine the widest range of subsequent consequences.

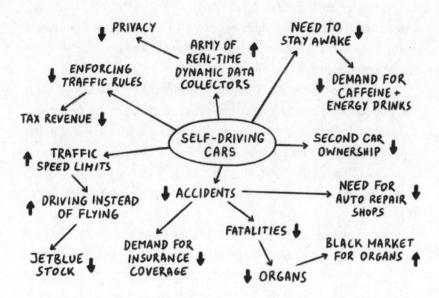

At this point, we're looking at a kind of messy wheel (to be honest, it looks more like a mind map than a wheel) that reveals some patterns and surprises. We would rank the consequences according to their likelihood of occurring and their potential impact. In this case, perhaps it's: 1) fewer fatalities, 2) more people driving instead of flying, and 3) higher taxes to pay for road maintenance.

Now strategies can be developed to capitalize on positive consequences and mitigate negative ones. Consider the most surprising implications and consider whether you might be looking at an opportunity to innovate. For example, maybe now would be a good time to develop a new kind of highway construction material so that the roads in the self-driving-car-future can charge electric car batteries.

When you use empathy to test drive potential scenarios and eventualities, you're creating a kind of menu of the choices you might make next. Think about the short- and long-term effect each scenario may have on your aspirations, values, and well-being. Evaluate the desirability and feasibility of these effects and consider the resources and skills required to take action. This is not quite a decision tree, but it does illuminate the choices that are worth considering.

Predictive empathy is also a kind of empathy for the future. Your human-centered and consequence-oriented thinking helps you anticipate the needs and experiences of the people who will live in the world you leave behind. It asks you to imagine their perspectives and consider their needs along with your own. There will be no "better world" for generations that follow yours without your empathy for the future.

Early in my career, I worked for Deloitte & Touche as a consultant on a funding project for women entrepreneurs in South Africa. From a tiny office in Cape Town, I took calls all day long from women looking for advice and funding to start their own businesses. They had a short window of time to take advantage of this opportunity, so I had to get a quick understanding of their personal circumstances and business objectives to be able to help them apply for this funding. It was like entrepreneurial speed dating.

Over four months, I assisted numerous women in creating business plans for ventures ranging from a coffee shop/art space to a twenty-four-hour fitness studio to a chicken farm that would supply products to large fast-food chains. My immersion in their personal stories and aspirations was intense and exhilarating. As I became familiar with the challenges of their experience as well as their hopes and ambitions, I found myself sharing their passion and excitement for their future.

Practicing empathy leads to personal growth by challenging you to see someone else's perspective and responding—sometimes just inside yourself—in a way that demonstrates your understanding. It's this new understanding that enriches your own perspective and makes it truer to and more encompassing of the diverse world you inhabit.

In the same way curiosity determines the shape of the many paths ahead of you, expansive empathy influences the depth and meaning of those paths. It contributes to your emotional clarity and sharpens your purpose so you're prepared to make the choices your future-ready mindstate tees up for you. It's the bridge between "I" and "you" (otherwise known as "we") that is a reminder at every turn that your future is experienced in the company of others. Make it work for both of you.

Do Human

Con-

nec-

tions

AMPLIFY

opportunity

for you?

Put your hand over your heart.

Remember something bold you did
entirely on instinct.

Think of the exhilaration you felt at
the time.

Did anything change because of what
you did?

CHAPTER 7

Your Dimension X

Dimension X is your unique superpower, the force that runs hot in you. It has a strong hand in what's happening to you right now as well as what your future will look like tomorrow.

You may have heard this question before: What advice would you give your sixteen-year-old self? Or how about this one: What do you wish you knew when you were twenty that you know now?

I know this is a popular way to package the "wisdom" of a person who has had a lot of experience or success and sell it to someone just starting out. But I don't get it. Why would I ask my older self what my younger self should have known or done? The missteps I've made or the odd turns I've taken are a) part of what makes me who I am and b) in the past. That train has not only left the station, it has arrived in the present (aka, the future, to my younger self). Offering someone else a road map of the pitfalls and speed bumps I experienced along the way offers them a defensive strategy, at best. No one will gain any yards by looking in *my* rearview mirror.

Recognizing your future-ready milestones is going to get you much further than fretting over even one of your mistakes. These milestones are the key moments and turning points—the highs *and* the lows—of your journey that influence your path forward. You can look at the future-ready milestones at any juncture in your life and see the events that shaped you and your distinctive responses to those events. This is a retrospective view that ends right where your future begins, which is a powerful reminder that the future—what happens next—is as close as the very next choice you make.

A quick sketch of my own future-ready milestones might look like this:

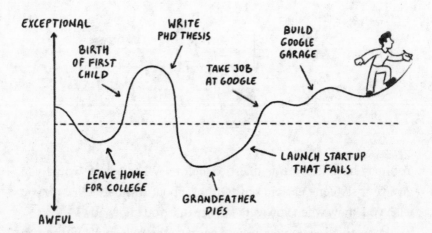

The first thing I notice when I look at these milestones is how neutrally I regard them now. As difficult as, say, my grandfather's death was for me when I was twelve, when I look at it in combination with other milestone events in my life, I can appreciate that it was pivotally important because it prompted me to let go of any excuse to move tentatively through my own life. It also triggered an intense need to see myself in the context of the whole world, not just in the place where I grew up. When I consider the birth of my first child, I remember great happiness, of course, but also clearly see it as a new and dynamic factor in my approach to my future. My choices became more complicated but at the same time more interesting, as I was now thinking about a family instead of just myself.

I can see another important factor revealed in my milestone map, a particular quality in me that has played a part in either bringing about these events or in coloring my responses to them. This quality—a strong bias for action—is what I call my "Dimension X." My own Dimension X is a default setting to just go for it without overthinking or overfocusing on consequences. I believe that there's no such thing as a perfect decision and that most of the time taking action helps me learn and adapt quickly. This bias for action also allows me to identify and take advantage of opportunities immediately as they arise. You know the phrase "jump at the chance"? I'm the jumper.

Almost every professional and educational opportunity I have ever had is the result of my bias for action. I applied for more than sixty visiting researcher positions to secure a spot at Stanford. I built the Google Garage without asking anyone for permission. Early in my career, this quality landed me in far-flung parts of the world, doing jobs I'd never considered before. Combined with the other dimensions (particularly openness and experimentation), my bias for action has enabled me to move fast and make choices—often risky ones—that have caused me to grow as a person. It has also been a turbo booster that hurtles me toward opportunities I would otherwise never have encountered.

Some of the big changes in our lives happen in an instant. Whether they're happy or devastating, it's easy to identify those momentous events. Other changes take place over a longer period of time and often we can't see or appreciate them until we've come out the other end and are well into another chapter. What makes any of these events a future-ready milestone—whether it was positive or negative—is the extent to which it precipitated your forward motion.

By now you know that radical optimism presents you with choices to see the better opportunities ahead of you. Unreserved openness lays out your choices to embrace the unknown. Compulsive curiosity offers you choices to seek and find the future. Perpetual experimentation produces choices to test and taste the future. Expansive empathy makes your choices more purposeful and life centered.

These dimensions of your future-ready mindstate help you see the choices available to you and enable you to shape your future with every choice you make. Your Dimension X influences your choices to make the future distinctly yours. Your Dimension X is unique to you and is the lens through which you see the world not as it is, but as you are (to gently paraphrase Anaïs Nin). Your Dimension X is the through line of the events of your life that move you forward. Over time, it becomes a signature reflex that plays an increasingly important role in shaping your future. Think of it as a strong, confident hand on the rudder as you make your way forward[1]—that's your Dimension X.

To make the most of your Dimension X, you should understand the role it plays in your overarching narrative as well as in your day-to-day stories. Then use it to make the impossible happen.

What Are Your Milestones?

Have a look at your own highs and lows. Think about the moments of your life that feel like they were significant junctures—individual events that caused you to have an emotionally intense response or longer-term developments that clearly mark a turning point or prompted profound learning or growth. These are often not the "big deal" moments you might think they'd be, such as a graduation or marriage or a promotion. Instead, it might be a subtle realization related to a personal relationship or an occurrence in your life.

On a blank piece of paper oriented horizontally, draw a line across the middle from side to side. The left edge of the page represents the earliest part of your life and the right edge represents where you are today. Positive experiences will appear above the line and negative experiences will appear below the line.

Graph five to ten milestone events across the page and include a brief description under each event. Look at the events on your map and consider these questions:

Do you remember your state of mind at the time these milestone events happened?

What actions did you take as a result of each event?

Can you identify something you learned from one event that affected your approach to the next event?

Was there a particular factor that influenced your response to these events or even prompted any of these events to occur?

You will likely spot something like a synapse at the point of your milestones, a connection with a bit of energy around it that indicates the presence of this factor. Maybe you remember how you made a decision at one of these times. Whether it was spontaneous or deliberate, you had clarity about your choice. It made sense to you because this factor was helping you express a truth about who you are and what you believe.

Your Dimension X intensifies over time and becomes intrinsic to the decisions you make that respond to or cause these milestone events. Former Googler Earth Chariyawattanarut grew up in Thailand but has lived and worked all over the world. His Dimension X—the ability to gain a deep insight into another person—has guided him through a maze of diverse experiences, opportunities, and challenges since he was a child. Early on, it helped him as the "new kid" to adapt to different circumstances and environments. But as he began to move through his career, he realized that being able to understand another person's point of view allows him to figure out what's important to them. This has been critical to his success in building partnerships and collaborations across organizations and industries. "For me, it's not a static trait," says Earth. "It's a dynamic process that's not just about understanding others; it's also about bringing people together and fostering unity in diversity."

You may not always be aware of how your Dimension X is shaping your path forward. Sometimes you wake up in the morning and realize, "Oh, hey, I'm somewhere else!" Or maybe you don't consciously associate your Dimension X with what's happening in the moment. Laura Jones is well acquainted with her strength, but she's still surprised by the places it takes her.

Making Surprising Connections

LAURA JONES

When I was in college, I took all the art classes and worked in a stage design shop, but because I was an economics major, it was kind of expected that I would go on to be a consultant or an investment banker. I went to work for Deloitte and quickly found myself living in hotel rooms and spending entire days in spreadsheets. I needed a creative outlet, so I found a studio where I could paint at night when I was not traveling. You'd think this would be satisfying, but it actually made it harder to accept this career path I was on. I realized that I would need to stop what I was doing and go find work that connected my analytical and creative sides to let me be my full self.

What came next was a bit of a soul-searching odyssey. I left Washington, DC, where I had been living, and came to San Francisco to go to business school at Stanford. I was also meeting with different people in hybrid business-creative fields, trying to get some sense of what might be out there for me. A friend told me about a new institute at Stanford that had something to do with design but was also about business and creativity—I was intrigued.

I wanted to talk to someone there and I discovered that this school wasn't even in a building, it was literally in a trailer with a plastic sign on the outside. I remember putting my hand on that trailer and thinking, *Whatever's inside this thing is my destiny.* And it was. The whole world of design thinking brought together all the threads of me. Besides helping to make sense of whatever my career path could be, I loved how it builds a sense of wide-open possibility into whatever you apply it to.

After business school, I went to work for Visa in marketing and strategy. Coming fresh from these incredibly stimulating creative experiences I had at school, my first day on the job I remember looking at my cubicle and the gray carpeting everywhere and wondering a little about what I'd gotten myself into. My first assignment was to take a stack of papers someone handed me and make a report on consumer insights for an upcoming all-hands meeting.

Well, if I learned anything at school, it was how to look at something and open myself to it being something completely different. I'm sure people were expecting a pretty straightforward deck with some charts and graphs. Instead, I took all the data and created an immersive POV video and set the whole presentation to music. Everyone was like, "What is this?" but in a great way. This moment was the beginning of the next chapter of my career where I was able to integrate all my learning and values and put them into practice.

After leaving Visa, I spent four years at Google, where I found an amazing outlet for my energy and ambition to learn more and have a greater impact. When Uber called me about a new opportunity, I was pregnant and comfortable at Google, and I wasn't sure I wanted to take a risk to do something I might fail at. But then I remembered that feeling I had outside the Stanford d.school trailer and I knew I had to go for it.

A certain strength that has often amplified my experience—my Dimension X—is the ability to make unexpected connections. I can visualize how an unconventional or counterintuitive connection between different people or ideas might lead to an opportunity that hasn't been considered. It's like having a palette with lots of colors in front of me and being able to see combinations that others might not. For example, at Google I connected fashion people with engineers to create shoppable videos. At Instacart, being able to speak the language of creatives, performance marketers, and data scientists lets me play with really interesting new ideas. This tends to mean that most days, I am doing something that I've never done before. One project I launched started with a memo I wrote and ended many connections and several months later with Lizzo in a bathtub in Prague, starring in an Instacart ad campaign that would debut during the 2022 MTV Video Music Awards. It was epic and surprising but also exactly what you'd hope for when you take the leaps in your life.

Your Dimension X will always remind you of what's possible, whether in high or low times. It's the kick in the pants that pushes you out of your comfort zone and into a danger zone (mostly the good kind of danger) that tests you and shows you what you're really capable of.

An organization's Dimension X is reflected in its culture. For example, the cultures at Tesla and SpaceX are defined by taking risks and learning from the wins and losses of iterative experimentation. Let's say "embraces failure" is their Dimension X. If you mapped the future-ready milestones of these two companies, you'd see the influence of this dimension at every juncture.

CEO Elon Musk has said, "If things are not failing, you are not innovating enough." When a spacecraft prototype crashes, Musk congratulates the SpaceX engineers for the data they've gathered. When customer feedback points to a flaw, Tesla engineers are eager to find the solution. Once a Tesla owner named Joe complained that the audio alerts in his car were so loud they frequently woke his sleeping baby. In its next software update, Tesla introduced "Joe Mode" to offer consumers a quieter alert option. Embracing failure has enabled the quick, continuous learning produced by perpetual experimentation that has driven these companies forward in their respective corners of the transport manufacturing industry.

Change Your Mindstate: COI

What you don't see in your milestone map are the events or periods where you didn't move forward or may even have moved backward. These instances are frequently the result of choosing not to act even though your Dimension X is encouraging you to do so.

Think about three different occasions in your life where you chose to do nothing instead of following your instincts. For each case, try to remember what held you back from taking action. What were the ultimate outcomes in these three situations? Were they the result of you not taking action? Were you satisfied with these outcomes?

Now for each case, imagine two different outcomes that might have occurred if you had taken action. Are those imaginary outcomes better than what actually happened? Do they align better with your values or aspirations?

The cost of inaction, or COI, will always be greater than the cost of making a mistake. The next time you find yourself hesitating to act, project ahead to those potential outcomes and ask yourself: *What would my Dimension X do?*

Take a Closer Look

If you think of your Dimension X as a recurring character in the long arc of your personal narrative, when you consider your experience in narrower slices, you can see the small ways it plays with the other dimensions of your future-ready mindstate. Think of a few days or a week recently where it felt like a lot happened. Maybe you had a big deliverable due at work or a friend was going through a personal crisis and needed your help.

Break down the days surrounding the event into several little pieces and map your experience as you did your highs and lows earlier. This time think about where the dimensions of your future-ready mindstate played a part in how things went down.

Say you have an opportunity to pitch a business idea to an investor. Here's how it might look:

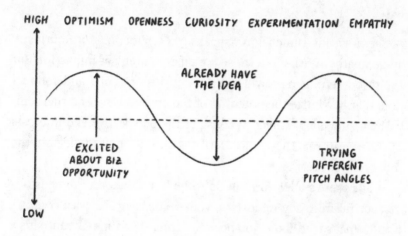

Understandably, you've got tons of optimism about this opportunity. Your openness and curiosity are less engaged, probably because you're so focused on this single thing and not scanning the horizon for other things. Your experimentation is helping you test different approaches as you prepare for your pitch presentation. Maybe your empathy is not high because you're thinking almost exclusively of yourself—you the funding hunter, the bootstrapper, the person with a big idea.

Now draw a line that represents where your Dimension X—in this case, let's say it's resourcefulness—shows up throughout this experience in relation to the other dimensions.

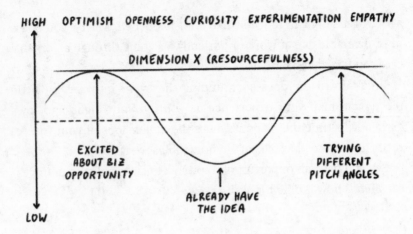

See how this Dimension X peaks in conjunction with curiosity and empathy? Without it, those dimensions aren't as impactful. But the resourceful person will use their curiosity to find and connect dots that maximize the potential of the opportunity. And their empathy would enable them to consider the perspective and interests of the investor so they can describe the promise of the idea in the most relevant terms.

While there's a lot you can do to build up the other dimensions of your future-ready mindstate, your Dimension X basically grows itself. What's true about you becomes truer over time. Because it's a strength, you think it's only doing you good. But it's such a powerful force there may be times when it will land you in uncomfortable situations or places you didn't mean to be.

Here's what I mean by this: Every summer, I return with my family to my hometown in Germany for Rutenfest, an annual festival that dates back to the seventeenth century. The five-day festival involves a lot of student award ceremonies, shooting competitions, and neighborhood gatherings, but the high point is a parade that draws tens of thousands of spectators every year. The parade participants include marching bands and musicians dressed in traditional costumes, and drumming groups representing all of the city's high schools, most notably a group called Tommlerkorps that I led the year I graduated from high school. This thirty-four-member drum corps has been around for more than 150 years, and it was a tremendous honor to be chosen by my fellow students to be a part of this group.

Not long before the festival in 2023, I learned from another alumnus that interest in participating in Tommlerkorps had been waning and that only twenty-two students would be performing that year, twelve fewer than usual. This hit me hard. I felt I had to do something about it, so just as the festival got underway, a friend and I wrote an op-ed for a local newspaper that proposed several new initiatives intended to preserve this historic entity by making the corps more inclusive and democratic. Among other things, we suggested admitting female students to the group for the first time, as well as investing in better instruments and costumes and promoting social engagement—all reasonable ideas that we hoped would get students excited about the group again.

That's not at all how things played out. For the duration of the festival and long after, there were hundreds of brutal comments against me and my friend on the newspaper's website, just really aggressive, threatening remarks telling us to quit picking on Tommlerkorps and to go back to California. I was stunned by this response, more so when even old school pals emailed me to end our friendship over the article.

I felt like a lifeguard diving into the pool to save someone from drowning, only to have the swimmer scream at me to leave them alone. It was a crazy few days that were entirely the result of my jumping into action out of my lifelong affection for this group. My regret isn't that I acted, it's that I acted without thinking harder about how people might react and that I didn't act years earlier when I was in a position to help the group think about the future. I know this to be true, however: if this group decided to experiment with new ideas and approaches, they would discover more opportunities and more opportunities would find them. No downside there!

You can't really hit the PAUSE button or otherwise call off your Dimension X. It's going to bring its intense force to just about everything of consequence that you do. Earth Chariyawattanarut says that sometimes he finds himself so tuned in to someone else that he starts to absorb their energy, which is fine when it's positive energy and not so fine when the person is negative or anxious. He has learned to pay attention when this happens and take steps to protect his own healthy state of mind.

Operate with an awareness of your Dimension X's influence on your thinking and behavior. Learn something—as I did—when it takes you into choppy waters. Then use that along with the other dimensions of your future-ready mindstate to make it back to dry land. Former Googler Sarah Deveraux's Dimension X has been a factor in some of her greatest challenges and accomplishments.

Using All Your Powers

SARAH DEVEREAUX

I grew up outside of Detroit, Michigan, in a family of blunt, tenacious, well-intentioned people who taught me to fight for what I believe. My grandmother was an environmental activist in the '60s, and I saw how hard she worked to get people to do the right thing. Finding common ground wasn't an option; she'd just keep hammering away at an issue from every angle until she just overpowered everyone. I get why she did it—it seemed more efficient, and the issues she was battling were urgent. But it wasn't the most effective approach.

Years later, I was running the g2g (Googler to Googler) program, Google's peer-to-peer learning network. I had been building the infrastructure for the program for about eight months when I got on a videoconference with my manager to tell him we were ready to scale the operation. I was expecting him to be really happy about the massive amount of work I'd done to get to this point so quickly, and I was pretty confident we'd be talking about a promotion for me. Instead, he said, "Sarah, you're great, but you're pushing too hard and you're pissing people off. I can't help you advance your career unless you seriously change your style and learn to bring people along with you."

At first I felt defensive and so sad that I knew I was going to cry. I had a great relationship with my manager, but not the kind where either of us would be comfortable with such a display of emotion. So I asked to end the call and talk the next day. Then I cried in the corner for a while, thinking about how I was always being told to push things forward as quickly as possible. *This is ridiculous,* I thought. *How am I supposed to do things differently if there's always so much time pressure?* I was surprised and hurt by this feedback, which seemed to come out of nowhere.

Then I thought of a moment a few years earlier when I was opening Google's Boston office, a time-crunch project where I had been working nonstop for three months straight. I pressed people pretty hard and stepped on quite a few toes to meet that deadline. I remembered the word "bulldozer" being used more than once to describe me, but I buried the thought at the time because I was so focused on the objective.

I trusted my manager, and I knew he was telling me the truth. So I made a decision to change. I basically created a development path for myself, asking people for advice and reading a lot and taking different courses. I struggled with the fact that managers had often tapped me for certain projects *because* I was a bulldozer and they knew I'd get the job done. At one point in my transformation journey, someone actually told me it seemed like I wasn't as productive anymore. I said, "Well, that's because I'm trying to accomplish things in a more patient and thoughtful way, and it's going to take me time to strike the right balance between productivity and perspective."

This was as hard as anything I've ever done. When something really needed to be accomplished quickly, I'd think, *This is an extenuating circumstance, so maybe I should let the old me handle the situation.* I had to keep reminding myself that I was never going to change how I operate in the world and have the impact I hoped for unless I became that future, better version of myself. It took me six long years to get to where I was able to approach problems and relationships with people in the way I wanted to—with mindful authenticity. I still don't show up the way others want or expect me to. I'm opinionated, forceful, and a little rough around the edges. But I'm also kind, compassionate, and curious about the experience of others. I'm still me—

head to toe—but I'm more mindful of the impact my perfectly imperfect self has on others.

I have far more satisfaction and joy in the coaching and facilitation work I do today. I am more curious and care more deeply about how I relate to other people. I moved back to Michigan a couple of years ago, and I feel a great sense of optimism, despite lately spending every waking hour calling every government agency and elected official I can think of about the Huron River water crisis in the southeastern part of the state. My husband said to me recently, "You're in a very good mood considering you're up against a multimillion-dollar corporation that's been polluting the water in Michigan for a decade." I think I feel optimistic because I'm reframing the challenge for myself and others as "Hey, let's use this crisis as a catalyst for innovation and for thinking differently about the future of the Great Lakes region."

It's interesting that my Dimension X—grit—was so intrinsic to my greatest growth challenge but also enabled me to overcome that challenge and find a more gratifying and impactful way to be in the world. Today I'm sure that creating something together with people I may not agree with is the only way to achieve sustainable progress. My grandmother would have gone to the mats with those same people, but I think making everything a fight is what's gotten us to this place where there's no meaningful dialogue and it's impossible to create positive change together.

I have a thing about not working in standard workspaces. For me, work is about dreaming and brainstorming and thinking of new things, so traditional desks feel very restrictive for my brain. When I was living in Colorado, I had this great stone-topped table in my kitchen that was my favorite place to work. When we were preparing to relocate from Colorado to Michigan, the movers we hired to help us with the big stuff dropped my table. I thought it was going to be okay, but when we unpacked it in Michigan, there was a huge crack down the center of the table.

I set it up in my new workspace, but every time I looked at the crack, I got irritated at the movers all over again for dropping the table. I kept telling my husband that we needed to order a new piece of stone for the top of the table because the crack was driving me crazy. One day he said, "Maybe you could just think of the crack as a reminder that we got through this difficult move and we're here, right where we're supposed to be." I thought, *Good job, Paul—excellent mindset shift*. Now every time I look at this crack, which runs the entire length of the table, I think, *Yeah, I can do it*. Show me the challenge and I will rise to it because I'm right where I'm supposed to be.

As you grow more aware of your Dimension X, you'll discover that you're tapping it more consciously and more frequently and its power is increasingly accessible to you. When I was considering launching a start-up while I was a researcher and PhD candidate at a university, I asked myself, *Go or no go?* I knew this venture would take a lot of time and resources, but I also knew from every other occasion when I had jumped to act that I would be changed by what I learned from the experience.

I was disappointed when my start-up failed, but I didn't feel weighed down by disappointment, I think because I was learning how to "land" when I leaped. I was also learning that my Dimension X wasn't always going to lead me to some dramatic breakthrough or giant success. It was reinforced by each experience, though, and over time, I got better and better at recognizing the next moment to act, in part due to the ongoing amplification of the other future-ready dimensions in me.

When your Dimension X is front of brain and, say, your openness or curiosity or empathy is peaking, the choices that present themselves to you will be clear and compelling.

Change Your Mindstate: Story

No matter how well you think you know yourself and your own narrative, you will always be surprised and enlightened by the way someone else describes you. Think of three people who play very different roles in your life—say, a partner or other family member, a colleague, and a friend. Ask them to tell you a story about you where they think your Dimension X had an impact. If needed, ask questions that surface details that help you appreciate how they perceive this strength in you. Even if they recount stories that are familiar to you, they may reveal a new insight about how others see you. You may even discover a milestone or two for your map that you hadn't thought of.

Square the Circle

There's a problem in geometry called "square the circle" that was first posed by the ancient Greeks, who wondered whether a square could be constructed with the same area as a circle using just a compass and ruler. After vexing mathematicians for hundreds of years, in the late 1800s, the Lindemann–Weierstrass theorem proved that this task could not, in fact, be accomplished. Since then, "square the circle" has become a metaphor for trying to do the impossible.

I love this phrase. It doesn't make me think of failure, it makes me think of the guts and initiative it takes to try to do something new and difficult that you know may not be possible. The idea that mathematicians stood at the blackboard and worked this problem for centuries, building on one another's thinking and shaking off self-doubt and disappointment, reminds me that everything I try to do today as just one person in this world may actually be part of a solution that is realized in the future. I may never see the fruit of my efforts, but I have an abundance of confidence that what I do has future impact. This is an essential aspect of being future ready: knowing that every choice I make has consequence, whether tomorrow or further down the road.

Larry Page used to say: "Have a healthy disregard for the impossible." Let your Dimension X help you do that. When you confront a challenge or an obstacle, your Dimension X will remind you of what you're capable of doing while the other dimensions of your future-ready mindstate will present you with the creative components to do something about it.

Listen to your Dimension X. It's your most powerful and reliable answer to resistance from outside forces or from within yourself. If you're hesitant to address a challenge, think back on those instances where your Dimension X changed the way things unfolded for you. It gave you confidence in the choices you made and ensured that you landed in a place of growth and learning. That's what makes it such an incredible asset when you have to do something hard.

In 2012, Stanford University launched the University Innovation Fellows program to engage college students from around the world in a vital conversation about the future of education. I was quick to get involved in the program because it promised to touch on my favorite subjects—innovation and education. Led by founder Leticia Britos Cavagnaro, the program creates change agents by offering participants training to drive innovation in education. Each of the 2,500-plus students who have participated in the program go home prepared to do the difficult work of making change. Leticia's Dimension X—what she describes as interdimensional thinking—provides them with a powerful way to understand what it takes to do this.

Leticia says that people often get stuck because they're not accustomed to moving between the conceptual and the practical. This ability amounts to having a concurrent sense of what's in the close-up and the long shot or how what's happening thirty minutes from now relates to the fundamental philosophy or purpose of what you've been doing for the last ten years. At one of the program's first annual meetups that I hosted at Google, I saw this evidenced in an uncanny way.

The 250-person event was taking place in a room that comfortably held maybe 200 people. The space was teeming with enthusiasm and ideas, which was exciting, but some of the basic logistics of the day were starting to seem unwieldy. Before the event began, we discussed how we would handle bathroom breaks. Leticia quickly scanned the room and said, "We can't do bathroom breaks. It will take forever for 250 people to get through the doors, and it will take just as long for them to wait in line to use the restroom and return to their seats. We'll announce that everyone should just take a bio break whenever they need to." In that instant, she assessed time and space and zoomed in on a critical detail that, if not anticipated, could easily have taken all the air out of the entire event.

The lesson for me was this: to solve a big problem (in this case, a 250-people-in-a-small-room problem), you have to have the capacity to see things from a high level without losing sight of the details. This is hard, but not impossible. Leticia has the unusual ability to do that all by herself—she moves fluidly between the telescope and the microscope views. The rest of us are able to do it if we're lucky enough to be part of a team or organization that values both of those perspectives.

Launching a start-up is one of the all-time gut-wrenchingly hard things to do. You're putting it all on the line—your idea, your reputation, your time, your money, other people's money—knowing that the odds are against your success. You can see why your Dimension X can be such an influential factor as you contemplate launching a start-up and, of course, after you take the plunge. It's also a singular competition differentiator that may not appear in your business plan but could well make the difference in the success of your start-up.

I saw this over and over again in my work with Google for Start-ups, an initiative launched in 2011 to support the development of local start-up communities around the globe. As part of this initiative, we launched "Designers of Innovations," a program where I worked with twenty Polish entrepreneurs to become lead facilitators to train other aspiring entrepreneurs in user-centered, prototype-driven innovation. The Polish government sponsored this effort in hopes of igniting the entrepreneurial potential of women across the country. More than five thousand people ultimately received this training, but one in particular inspires me to this day.

Malgorzata was a project manager in a large industrial plant. She had inherited her grandparents' stone farmhouse and wanted to turn it into a consumer attraction and experience that focused on environmental protection and education, specifically the concept of zero waste. Her ability to execute was the Dimension X she brought to her day job, but she was struggling to articulate a viable business concept for her start-up. The program helped her use empathy to understand what a consumer's environmental aspirations might be, as well as how they would use the various aspects of the experience she envisioned. Once her idea took on this user-centric focus, she could see right away how to build it.

The farm is now a tourist destination that's part of Natura 2000, a network of sites that aims to conserve biodiversity across Europe. The property features solar panels, a bicycle trolley, and a bird-watching workshop in an old barn. In the works are an instructional bread-baking space, a sewing workshop for repurposing old clothes, an herbarium, and an educational farm for children. Her empathy for her future guests and her make-it-happen Dimension X allowed Malgorzata to express her environmental values in an extraordinary way.

The question I like a lot better than "What would I tell my younger self?" is "What can I do today to create a new opportunity for myself tomorrow?" The answer is simple: make just one brand-new choice today. That choice will open a little door and tomorrow you will be exploring what was behind the door. Your Dimension X will ensure that your choice is interesting, maybe even a little edgy, and that you're pointed ahead toward your future.

Your Dimension X is right there with you all the time, ready to give you a nudge toward the future you're crafting. It's your signature, your fingerprint, the singular thing that's true about you. Use it to make the big, bold moves. And use it to make quiet decisions that have far-reaching impact.

Do you

RISE

opport

to meet

unity?

CHAPTER 8

A Day in the Life of Future- Ready You

Every page of this book is meant to stimulate the dimensions of your future-ready mindstate and make you realize the potential inside you, all around you, and ahead of you. You should be feeling very close to your own realm of possibility right now. You don't know what your future will be, but you know it doesn't have to just happen to you. It's something you can actively create, day by day, with every choice you make.

Picture a composer sitting down at the piano to write a score. Inspired by an idea, they jot down a couple of bars, play the notes, tinker with them, then add some more. In an ongoing act of creativity and imagination, the music takes shape through the countless choices they explore. Tapping every dimension of their future-ready mindstate—optimism, openness, curiosity, experimentation, and empathy—the composer is fashioning something new and—thanks to their Dimension X—unique to their experience and perception of the world.

That composer is you, creating your future.

This makes you hop out of bed every day, excited to discover where the music will take you. You're no longer just putting one foot in front of the other, trying to avoid change and uncertainty. You're making a future that embraces a vast spectrum of possibilities. No longer bound by the constraints of doubt or fear, you craft your journey with eager anticipation. Your imagination points you to the real places you want to be and experiences you want to have. Every choice you make and every challenge you overcome adds depth and texture to the unfolding composition—your future.

Live Future Ready

Every day I strive to live future ready. This means I keep the future close so I can see the opportunities that are immediately in front of me. I also nurture my vision of the future out on the horizon so that I will aim high every time I make a choice. I don't know what will happen, but I am prepared to thrive wherever the path toward the future goes.

When you live future ready, you are prepared to leverage inevitable change to your advantage. You are poised to realize the power of everyday choices to shape your future. You recognize that the future is an ongoing journey of awareness, learning, and adaptation, not a destination, and you are able to envision and anticipate the opportunities that the future holds.

To live future ready is to continuously cultivate an outlook of possibility and resilience that transforms apprehension about the unknown into excitement about what may happen next. Your optimism focuses you on what could go right instead of what might go wrong. Your openness makes change your friend. Curiosity moves you to explore and seek to understand ideas that are new to you. When you experiment, fear of failure transforms into the thrill of learning and discovery. Empathy reminds you you're not alone and expands your sense of collective possibility. And your Dimension X threads itself through your experience to make big things happen.

Whatever good you do for yourself or for the world will happen because you were ready to take action when you saw the chance. On any given day, the dimensions of your future-ready mindstate present you with multiple opportunities to act on behalf of your own future. With creativity and imagination, you consider the choices before you and make them with confidence. You don't know where each choice will land you, but you know you will land and you will be prepared to make the next choice.

Take tomorrow, for example. What choices might you make tomorrow that open new veins of discovery? Consider what you expect will happen: You'll do things you need to do (walk the dog, eat breakfast, work), and you'll do things you want to do (read a book, go to the gym, make popcorn after dinner). You'll also respond to things that you couldn't anticipate, stuff that just happens (it rains, you get into a fender bender at a stoplight, you get a call from a former colleague). Within each of those ordinary activities and situations, there are multiple opportunities for future-ready you to make choices that may seem innocuous in the moment but are actually some of the notes you're sampling as you compose your future.

Any of these moments become possibility when future-ready you asks: *What if?* This simple question is the prism of your future-ready mindstate that colors your choices and infuses them with potential. So tomorrow, what if you have a brief conversation with a stranger that triggers a breakthrough idea? What if you take a walk during your lunch hour and hear a street musician playing a song that lifts you up? What if you read a poem that causes you to see a nagging problem in a completely different way? Everything that might happen tomorrow as you make each choice has the potential to transform the mundane into the extraordinary and become a new step into the satisfying future you're shaping for yourself. Because what's next is now.

How Do You Want to Be?

Your future-ready mindstate drives you to continuously learn, adapt, innovate, and connect with people and your environment in ways that evolve you toward your future. It pushes you to walk paths fueled by your aspirations and ensures you're equipped to navigate the complexities of whatever lies ahead. On this journey, it's not a question of what you want to do or who you want to be. It's a question of HOW you want to be.

This really is the heart of it: How do you want to be in your future?

How you are in your future will determine the impression—the "you-print"—that you will leave on this planet that's proof of your life. Will your you-print show what you believed in and what inspired you? Will it show that you were resilient and bold? Or that you tried to understand yourself and others? Will it show the positive impact you had on the people in your story? Or that you were fulfilled by the experiences your choices led you to?

Check in with yourself every day to make sure that how you are in this world is as you intend to be. There's no ideal "how to be" in your future. Like your Dimension X, it will be a perfectly distinctive expression of everything that's true about you. And if the choices you make each day reflect how you want to be, the future you build will be an appropriate legacy to how you lived your life. Because after all is said and done, it's how you are that people think about when you leave the room.

Living future ready—with optimism, openness, curiosity, experimentation, and empathy—is exactly what you need to make your own future. Are you ready?

Are you

FUTU

READY
for
your
RE?

Acknowledgments

So many people want to talk about the good old days and the past. I wanted to explore how to transition from preservation thinking to creation thinking, which is essential to shaping a better future, one that makes everyone a little happier and at home in this world. The journey of writing this book was only possible because I had the unwavering support of my family, friends, and colleagues and the institutions that gave me room to grow and experiment. Each of you has played a pivotal role in helping me envision and craft a future that unfolds every day in the most amazing way. In the end, writing this book was easy because all of you who have inspired me made it easy. I am grateful for your encouragement to sit down in my geodesic dome and start writing.

To my family, thank you for your endless love and encouragement. You are the foundation upon which this work stands. Thanks also for your patience as I have tested so many practices on you!

Mom, thank you for your love and support, always embracing life's challenges with an open heart and mind—and for being the most Internet-savvy *oma* I know.

Dad, thank you for your gentle guidance and for showing me how to cherish the beauty of life's traditions and joys.

Steffi, you helped me grow up by expanding my thinking. Our bond is unbroken by the oceans between us.

Anna, for being the grandmother whose nurturing spirit raised not only a family but also a legacy, always prioritizing the needs of others even in the toughest times.

Anne, for your easy nature and unforgettable laugh.

Benedikt, for your deep-rooted dedication to community.

Christiane, for keeping our family connected.

Dominik, for your entrepreneurial spirit and your approach to forging different paths.

Edith, your curiosity and gentle nudging about my book's progress have been a motivating force in my journey.

Elisabeth, for being a passionate teacher who has dedicated your life to special education.

Elisabeth, for showing us how to live a long, healthy life.

Erika, for building a remarkable legacy from scratch, generously enabling us to reap the benefits of your hard work and resilience.

Evelyn, for being a spiritual inspiration and setting your personal sails with mindfulness and grace.

Gregor, for being a doctor who practices with exceptional care and a heartfelt dedication to your patients.

Harald, who passed too soon, your lessons in navigating life's turbulent waves with a captain's mindset were instrumental in shaping my resilient outlook.

Helene, an educator with heart who embodies the right values in everything you do.

Hubert, for instilling in me a profound love for the forest.

Johannes, for your powerful thoughts on economics and the circular economy.

Jürgen, for your mechanical wisdom and talent in restoring classic machines, preserving them for future generations.

Karin, for being a teacher who deeply understands your students.

Konstanze, for the beautiful music you share with the world.

Laurenz, for your infectious, joyous enthusiasm for sports.

Lilli, for your commitment to caregiving and embodying the kindness and understanding our world so deeply needs.

Louis, for your inspirational approach to living with a more relaxed and composed perspective.

Maximilian, for standing up for what's right.

Rainer, for cherishing our family heritage and making a meaningful impact through your engagement in community work and politics.

Rainer, for being a true pillar of local entrepreneurship and running with all the best crazy ideas.

Robert, for your global business acumen and dedication to your own hometown.

Sabrina, for your warmth and care that enriches our family circle.

Sebastian, for being a teacher who exemplifies endurance, inspiring your students with persistence and resilience.

Valentin, for your skill and creativity as an architect, shaping our spaces in the world with vision and precision.

Wilhelm, for tirelessly advocating for the voice of the people in the realm of politics and showing me how to lead with empathy.

To my friends and colleagues, your influence on this project and on my life cannot be overstated. Each of you has contributed uniquely and significantly.

Alexander, for turning your hobby into a profession by mastering the art of brewing—lucky you.

Alfonso, for being a part of our first Airbnb experience and making Finland a cherished place.

Andrea, for sharing an office during times when writing was easy and when it was hard.

Andrew, for sharing your inflatable mattress for months during college and making memories as we discovered the California lifestyle.

Arne, for sharing my academic journey and creating our unusual mentorship guide together.

Astro, for making audacious moonshots real.

Benny, for your decades of friendship and teaching me the art of patience and the wisdom of slow steps.

Bernadette, for your zen approach to academia that blends tranquility with scholarly rigor.

Bernie, for showing us how to make achievement a habit.

Bill, for bringing important ideas to life with your gift for visual storytelling.

Bill, for making mindfulness and well-being a personal priority for us all.

Bobby, for generously imparting your love of animation to a world that needs exactly that.

Brad, for leading and inspiring communities with your deep values.

Christian, for demonstrating the art of working smarter, not harder, and paving the way to the career you've always envisioned.

Christian, for never missing an opportunity for a good gathering and making even a bad one seem fun.

Christian, for your AI innovations that pave the way for future exploration in technology and self-discovery.

Christoph, for your graciousness and warm hospitality, which have enriched the lives of so many.

Cristobal, for steering the E-Ship initiative and taking me to the end of the world.

Dan, for your invaluable advice and inspiration.

Daniel, for masterfully organizing the best trips.

Daniel, for our shared love of craft beer and your realism that reminds me to stay connected to the tangible world.

David, for being an extraordinary executive coach who left this world too soon.

David, for making design thinking accessible to everyone.

Debbe, for sharing stories that empower every designer.

Debbie, for always showing compassion to those who need it the most.

Derk, for setting an example of determination and strength every day.

Dong, for your neuroscience guidance and fun brainstorms about what futures could be.

Elle, for being my oldest friend and offering a model for navigating life authentically and with an open heart.

Emma, for our road trips with pipe cleaners and Play-Doh.

Erica, for being an exceptional manager.

Fabio, for your joyful eagerness to spend time together.

Flo, for maintaining a positive, stoic spirit even in the most challenging times.

Franziska, for your endlessly infectious positive spirit.

Frede, for your trust and support, every day in every way.

Gary, for believing in the future of education and providing a space for experimentation.

Georg, for your human kindness and empathy, which have been a guiding light for so many.

Gerow, for teaching me and my family that our imperfections add character and beauty.

Gisela, for showing us how to be open to everything.

Gordon, for being a true friend in good and bad times and for your grounded nature that proves balanced living is possible.

Hasso, for investing in a grand idea and me.

Hugo, for believing in the power of technology in education.

Hui Soo, for your enduring support and always pushing the envelope in education.

Humera, for nurturing and launching so many global changemakers.

Jan, for pulling me up every hill behind your back wheel.

Jan, for your passionate advocacy of cultural change.

Jana, for your unwavering commitment to finding the right talent.

Jens, for the memories created in the sand and snow.

Jens, for the unforgettable adventures in South Africa and the thrill of racing beetles together.

Jens, for helping to save the German economy and some good Konstanz times.

Jeremy, for transforming so many leaders into designer thinkers.

Jess, for your unshakable belief in the human heart.

Jörg, for helping me discover the future of mobility and its endless possibilities.

Jürgen, for advocating for human rights around the world and helping the powerless find their powers.

Karl-Heinz, for your enduring passion for education.

Katharina, for sharing a picture every day and our vision for temporary communities.

Katharina, for your endless optimism, creative spirit, and passion for pens.

Kay, for supporting my voice.

Keren, for your masterful communication to so many.

Klaus, for showing us how to stay true to ourselves.

Larry, for your 10x vision and shaping the future of a company everyone loves to work for.

Larry, for so kindly introducing me to the Stanford design community.

Lars, for being a truly reliable friend and sharing my love for sake.

Laszlo, for nudging HR into the future at Google.

Laurenz, for your valuable insights into the needs and perspective of the next generations.

Laurie, for spreading the Stanford Innovation Fellows magic around the world.

Léa, for being a powerful and eloquent advocate in shaping the future of AI.

Leticia, for a decade of monthly creative endeavors and inspiring generations as an educator par excellence.

Lilli, for your commitment to social work and serving as a role model for your generation.

Lisa, for teaching futures thinking to the leaders of today and tomorrow.

Louie, for being a learning design magician.

Lukasz, for your pivotal role in bringing Creative Skills of Innovation to over 10,000 aspiring entrepreneurs in Poland.

Lyra, for reimagining HR and the future of work.

Maks, for your optimism about the AI future.

Mamie, for finding and cofounding The Garage.

Marc, for inspiring generations of local family entrepreneurs.

Martin, for being a champion of fair trade coffee and those unexpected 3 a.m. calls.

Matthias, for frequent visits to our dome and making communication seem effortless.

Maureen, for your pioneering spirit in our teaching adventures.

Melissa, for providing access to mental health education for children.

Michael, for creating beautiful spaces for everyone.

Michi, for being a chef whose extraordinary food I wish everyone could taste.

Miriam, for leading Germany into a better digital future and proving that it's possible to invent tomorrow today.

Moritz, for being the pathfinder in remote places, leading where maps end.

Nico, for your adventurous lifestyle and passion for personal health.

Nina, for being a brand wizard and a wonderful friend who always shares good advice.

Ole, for being a great speaking coach with a design heart.

Oliver, for caring so much about more than winning.

Oliver, for your financial boldness and Swabian thrift, the secret to your success.

Oliver, for creating an ecosystem the founders of the future can thrive in.

Pascal, for your radical thoughts about the future.

Patrick, for being a true friend and cherishing traditions, even when we agree to disagree on them.

Peter, for your invaluable academic and life wisdom.

Philipp, for countless memorable evenings during stopovers in Frankfurt that helped me see that wherever I am with a good friend is home.

Rachel, for trying to find the good in all things.

Ralf, for spotting so many opportunities for a great story.

Ruchika, for your mindfulness and advocacy—you're a beacon of tranquility and wisdom.

Ryan, for being such a voracious learner.

Sarah, for leading the d.school and helping students to navigate the ambiguous future.

Scott, for making prototyping accessible to anyone.

Scott, for your creative genius and helping to make space for everyone.

Seamus, for being the creative spirit with an orange beanie, painting life in vibrant hues.

Sebastian, for being a wonderful friend whose companionship and support remain strong, despite the many miles between us.

Sergey, for remaining a visionary beyond Google and your casual inquiries about lost sunglasses.

Stefan, for the endless bike rides and teaching me how visual identity is shaped.

Stefan, for the myriad of memories shared in Konstanz, especially our conversation on that bench before our first college exam.

Stefan, for your reflective attitude that helps us see things more deeply.

Steffi, for inspiring so many kids to trust their creativity.

Steffi, for sparking my enthusiasm for Tesla's mission and heroically raising a family singlehandedly.

Stephanie, for being the superhero everyone should be so lucky to have on their team.

Tatjana, for caring so much about everyone and everything.

Thomas, for being a designer with remarkable vision.

Thomas, for being the actor everyone wants to call a friend.

Thomas, for your creative facilitation of Project Reimagine.

Thomas, for your journalist's heart and making me a little famous for just a moment.

Tim, for being a steadfast friend during our times of discovery in China.

Tim, for showing us how to change by design.

Tina, for teaching me so much about how to teach well and how to push good ideas into the world.

Tobias, for the all-night brainstorming sessions and telling stories around a fire with an infinity of stars above us.

Torsten, for your invaluable tech and idea support, and for being a cherished friend of a friend.

Tyler, for your artistic vision and giving everyone the feeling of being enough.

Ulf, for being the brand steward and creative power.

Uli, for championing design thinking in Germany.

Uli, for teaching me the art of perspective and the elegance of judo.

Vanessa, for holding down the fort and providing unwavering support as we chased new ideas in the desert.

Zoe, for your insightful perceptions about our conversations.

To Google and Stanford University, I will be forever grateful to have been a part of the most inspiring environment for humans to grow and build the future. Driving back and forth on the 101 between these two institutions to teach what I practice and practice what I teach allowed me to discover my own future.

Googlers/former Googlers, for your incredible stories in this book that prove we can create our own remarkable futures.

All the CSI:Lab evangelists, for helping me teach tens of thousands of Googlers how to build the future.

Stanford colleagues, for teaching me how to design a human-centered future.

To all my champions and partners in the publishing journey: Thank you for helping to bring this book—and all my hopes for every reader's future—into the world.

Hollis, for believing in this book.

Karen, for your creative genius that made not only this book but also a better future possible. Thank you for inspiring every page.

Francesco, for seeing what I was saying in the most elegant and insightful way.

Amanda, for your unwavering commitment to delivering this message to hearts and minds.

Leslie, for your remarkable dedication and results-driven approach.

Rachel, for shepherding this book through all the mysterious byways of the publishing process.

Janet, for your invaluable expertise in copyediting, which greatly enhanced the quality of the book.

Jessica, for being a PR partner who excels not only in understanding how to make a meaningful impact but also in effectively spreading the word.

Finally, to all whose lives I've had the privilege to touch, thank you for the invaluable lessons each of you has taught me along the way.

And to the future, I pledge to give my best in every moment, striving to make each chapter the brightest yet.

Notes

Chapter 1: The Future and You

1. On metaphors for the future: Draper L. Kaufman, *Teaching the Future: A Guide to Future-Oriented Education* (Palm Springs, CA: ETC Publications, 1976).
2. On the nature of creativity: Mihaly Csikszentmihalyi, *Creativity: Flow and the Psychology of Discovery and Invention* (New York, NY: Harper Perennial, 1996).

Chapter 2: Radical Optimism

1. On learned optimism: Martin E. P. Seligman, *Learned Optimism: How to Change Your Mind and Your Life* (New York, NY: Alfred A. Knopf, 2006).
2. Kelly Leonard and Tom Yorton, *Yes, And: How Improvisation Reverses "No, But" Thinking and Improves Creativity and Collaboration—Lessons from the Second City* (New York, NY: Harper Business, 2015).
3. Google Trekker photo from atop the Himalayas: Roberto Baldin, "Behold: Google's Stunning Street Views from the Top of the World," Wired, March 18, 2013, https://www.wired.com/2013/03/google-summit-maps/.
4. Charles and Ray Eames's *Powers of Ten* design film: https://youtu.be/ofKBhvDjuyo.
5. Kalle Ryan's song "My Blood Is Boiling for Ireland": https://youtu.be/3pJrsxpwJjE.

Chapter 3: Unreserved Openness

1. On openness and creativity: Joy Paul Guilford, "Creativity," *American Psychologist* 5, no. 9 (1950): 444–54, https://doi.org/10.1037/h0063487.
2. On openness and the state of "flow": Mihaly Csikszentmihalyi, *Flow: The Psychology of Optimal Experience* (New York, NY: Harper Perennial, 1991).
3. Oliver Bierhoff's "golden goal": https://youtu.be/Hyec44LVr38.
4. How to build a paper airplane: https://youtu.be/G7ec7qCHwzc.

Chapter 4: Compulsive Curiosity

1. On curiosity and creativity: George Land and Beth Jarman, *Breakpoint and Beyond: Mastering the Future Today* (San Francisco, CA: Harper Business, 1992).
2. On curiosity and child development: Susan Engel, *The Hungry Mind: The Origins of Curiosity in Childhood* (Cambridge, MA: Harvard University Press, 2015).
3. Swim with a whale shark: https://youtu.be/mn5a3XJhJd4?si=HXOCC8VZqtaZVnyA.
4. On questions and curiosity: Erwin Straus, "Man: A Questioning Being," *Tijdschrift Voor Philosophie* 17e, no. 1 (1955): 48–74, http://www.jstor.org/stable/40879945.

Chapter 5: Perpetual Experimentation

1. On experimentation and innovation: Mark Stefik and Barbara Stefik, *Breakthrough: Stories and Strategies of Radical Innovation* (Cambridge, MA: MIT Press, 2004).
2. On psychological safety in teams: Amy Edmondson, *The Fearless Organization: Creating Psychological Safety in the Workplace for Learning, Innovation, and Growth* (Hoboken, NJ: Wiley, 2018).
3. On design change and human behavior: Richard H. Thaler and Cass R. Sunstein, *Nudge: Improving Decisions about Health, Wealth, and Happiness* (New Haven, CT: Yale University Press, 2008).

Chapter 6: Expansive Empathy

1. On evolution and empathy: Frans de Waal, *The Age of Empathy: Nature's Lessons for a Kinder Society* (New York, NY: Harmony Books, 2009).
2. On empathy and emotional intelligence: Daniel Goleman, *Emotional Intelligence: Why It Can Matter More Than IQ* (New York, NY: Bantam Books, 1995).

Chapter 7: Your Dimension X

1. On leveraging your strengths: Marcus Buckingham and Donald O. Clifton, *Now, Discover Your Strengths* (New York, NY: The Free Press, 2001).

Index

risk and, 46, 47, 144
saying "yes," 26–27, 28, 29–30, 32–33
saying "yes" to yourself, 31–32
trust and, 46, 71
"yes, and" approach, 34–38
"yes, but" approach, 33–34

Page, Larry, 35–36, 63, 208
partnerships, and future-ready mindstate, xxiii
past
  imagination focused on, 14, 15
  patterns of, xix, 3
Pferdt, Angela, 74, 97, 110–11, 119–20
Pichette, Patrick, 64
Pixar Animation Studios, Braintrust meetings of, 128–29
Powers of Ten (film), 40
Prinz, Birgit, 58
problems
  as opportunities, xxiii
  reframing of, 41–44
prototyping 135–41, 144, 146

questions
  curiosity and, 109–13
  experimentation and, 126

Ratcliffe, Jon, xiv–xv, 106, 107–9, 138–39
reframing, and optimism, 38–44, 46, 47
resilience
  of future-ready mindstate, 217
  of optimists, 23
  uncertainty and, 28
risk
  curiosity and, 109
  experimentation and, 47, 123, 125, 129, 133, 138, 141–46
  openness and, 65, 67
  optimism and, 46, 47, 144
rituals, and openness, 58, 64, 80
Rogger, Daniel, 178
Rutenfest experience, 200–202
Ryan, Kalle, xv, 44, 45–46

Sandra By Design, xii
Schnellbüegel, Isabelle, xv, 27, 28–29
senses
  curiosity and, 92, 96–102
  engagement of, 32, 97–101
Sequoia Capital, 88
Shakespeare, William, 94

sharing, and openness, 72–76
Shunryu, 80
situational objectivity, 44
SpaceX, 197
Stanford d.school, 10–11, 37, 57, 111, 141, 149
Stanford University Innovation Fellows program, 208–9
Stark, Philippe, 161
start-ups, 87–88, 209–10
status quo bias, 54–55
The Strategy Collective, xv
Strauss, Erwin, 110
Street View technology, 35–36
superpower, Dimension X as, 6, 192, 211, 219

Tesla, 197–98
transparency
  authenticity and, 65–66
  openness and, 63–66
trust
  openness and, 6, 53, 63, 64, 65, 67–69, 71
  optimism and, 46, 71
  sharing and, 73
Tse, Raphael, xvi, 78
Tutu, Desmond, 108–9

Uber, 169–70, 196
uncertainty
  experimentation and, 143
  of future, xviii, xxii, xxiii, 2, 3, 5
  openness and, 54, 56, 59, 63
  resilience and, 28
United Nations, 46–47
unknown
  curiosity and, 92, 102–6
  experimentation and, 121, 124, 129, 144, 150
  not having answers, 107–9
  openness and, 60, 68
  optimism and, 22, 25
User Experience (UX), 175–77

Visa, 196

Weber, Astrid, xvi, 174, 175–77
wonder, state of, 105

YouTube, 170–71

zone of proximal development, 62

About the Author

DR. FREDERIK G. PFERDT helped shape one of the most fabled creative cultures in the world as Google's first Chief Innovation Evangelist. There he founded the Creative Skills for Innovation (CSI) Lab and The Garage, where tens of thousands of Googlers have been trained to imagine and experiment with new ideas. He also taught groundbreaking classes on innovation, creativity, and design at Stanford University for more than a decade.

His practices for living future ready are used by businesses, governments, nonprofit organizations, and entrepreneurs worldwide. He has been called "Dr. Innovation" and the "Pope of Creativity" in some of the more than 250 media outlets that have featured his work, including *Fast Company*, *Harvard Business Manager*, *Der Spiegel*, and BBC News. Born in Germany and educated globally, he experiments with a nature-centric lifestyle with his family in Santa Cruz, California.